This We Believe
QUESTIONS and ANSWERS

Richard L. Gurgel

NORTHWESTERN PUBLISHING HOUSE
Milwaukee, Wisconsin

Third printing, 2006
Second printing, 2006

Scripture is taken from the HOLY BIBLE, NEW INTERNATIONAL VERSION®. NIV®. Copyright © 1973, 1978, 1984 by International Bible Society. Used by permission of Zondervan. All rights reserved.

The "NIV" and "New International Version" trademarks are registered in the United States Patent and Trademark Office by International Bible Society. Use of either trademark requires the permission of International Bible Society.

Library of Congress Control Number: 2005921295
Northwestern Publishing House
1250 N. 113th St., Milwaukee, WI 53226-3284
www.nph.net
© 2006 by Northwestern Publishing House
Published 2006
Printed in the United States of America
ISBN: 978-0-8100-1743-6

Contents

Section I.
GOD AND HIS REVELATION

1. We believe that there is only one true God (Isaiah 44:6). He has made himself known as the triune God, one God in three persons. This is evident from Jesus' command to his disciples to baptize "in the name of the Father and of the Son and of the Holy Spirit" (Matthew 28:19). Whoever does not worship this God worships a false god, a god who does not exist. Jesus said, "He who does not honor the Son does not honor the Father, who sent him" (John 5:23).

Q: Since there are so many religions and different *gods* in each religion, how can we be confident that our God is the true God?

A: As you study the teachings of world "religions," it soon becomes evident that Christianity is unique. All other religions are based on man's best guesses with the guidance of only nature and conscience. In one way or another those religions put the burden on us to earn our own salvation with God. For example, the Muslim worshiper strives to give Allah obedience (*Islam* means "submission" or "obedience"). The Buddhist monk seeks to rise above this world's evils by his devotion to meditation. All other world religions ask sinners to make themselves right with God by their own efforts.

On the other hand, Christianity alone offers a completely different solution. Only Christianity teaches that being right with God is God's gift to us, not man's gift to God. Only Christianity teaches that God became man, not to teach us how to rise to him but to lift us up by his grace to himself. Christianity is not just one selection among many similar entrees on the world's religious smorgasbord. Its unique message testifies to its unique origin—a miraculous revelation by the true God. God has revealed the one saving truth that "no eye has seen, no ear has heard, no mind has conceived . . . but God has revealed it to us by his Spirit" (1 Corinthians 2:9,10).

Finally, the Holy Spirit himself works through the Word to convince us that the God who inspired Scripture is the one true God. Because this God gives us forgiveness and eternal life, we trust that his words are reliable and true.

Q : Was God *triune* even before the birth of Jesus?

A : Both the Old Testament—written before the birth of Christ—and the New Testament—written after Jesus' life, death, and resurrection—are consistent in teaching that there is only one true God. Both teach not only that God is one but that he is three persons within that one God. Certainly the teaching of the triune nature of God is expressed more fully in the New Testament, but the Old Testament had sufficient revelation of this truth for believers of that day to know it and believe it.

For instance, Jesus did not have to explain to the Jews of his day that there was a son of God since passages, such as Psalm 2:7 and Psalm 110:1, had already shared this truth with them. Their problem was not the concept of a son of God. They just refused to believe that Jesus was the Son of God. When Jesus spoke of the Holy Spirit, no one wondered what he was talking about. Old Testament passages, such as Genesis 1:2 and Isaiah 42:1, had clearly established the existence of the Holy Spirit.

God, from all eternity, has been and will continue to be one God, who has also revealed himself as Father, Son, and Spirit. While the word *triune* or *trinity* is not found in either the Old or New Testament, the truth that God is one and yet three is eternal. After his conception and birth the second person of the Trinity, the eternal Son of God took our human flesh and blood. God did not suddenly have a Son at Christmas, but rather the eternal Son revealed himself to the world in flesh and blood clothing.

Q: **How can we explain the Trinity as three persons and yet one God in a way that makes sense?**

A: God is absolutely unique. We can make no perfect comparison between him and anything we have seen or experienced in this world. Nothing created can adequately illustrate the uncreated triune God to the satisfaction of the human mind. In fact, all who insist upon making sense of the Trinity either end up with *three* gods or reduce Christ and the Holy Spirit to things less than God (such as in the teachings of the Jehovah's Witnesses).

God has revealed to us a wondrous glimpse of who he is, not to satisfy our curiosity so that we can make sense of him but to save us. Should it really surprise us that there are truths about our infinite God that go beyond our human understanding? For example, the difference between God and us is infinitely greater than the difference between a parent and a young child. The best response is to simply marvel at the wonder of God's essence and nature like a small child. A small child does not understand a parent but, in the best situation, simply trusts in the care and protection of that parent. We confess with the psalmist, "My heart is not proud, O LORD, my eyes are not haughty; I do not concern myself with great matters or things too wonderful for me. But I have stilled and quieted my soul; like a weaned child with its mother" (Psalm 131:1,2).

Are we unloving or intolerant when we proclaim that everyone who does not worship the triune God is actually worshiping a false god or a god who does not exist?

James tells us, "Remember this: Whoever turns a sinner from the error of his way will save him from death and cover over a multitude of sins" (5:20). We do not label a parent as unloving who points out danger to children. To point out an error in belief that could eventually condemn someone to an eternity apart from God is neither unloving nor intolerant. In fact, it can save someone from eternal death.

On the Last Day, every person who has ever lived or is living is going to bow before Jesus of Nazareth and confess him to be the true God and Lord (Philippians 2:10,11). Those who have believed in him will do this with joy and delight. Those who have not known him or have rejected him will do this with terror and sadness. How important it is that we share the simple truth that Jesus spoke in John 17: "Now this is eternal life: that they may know you, the only true God, and Jesus Christ, whom you have sent" (verse 3). On that Last Day, no one will label as unloving or intolerant the truth that there is no other God than the triune God. It will simply be clear to everyone as the truth that gives eternal life.

Couldn't God have revealed himself to different peoples in different ways and by different names?

The assumption behind this question is that all the different religions of the world teach basically the same thing.

They just call God by different names. This assumption also believes that religion is essentially nothing more than a set of good moral rules to live by in order to make God happy. In that sense, most world religions do have much in common. But God says something different in Scripture. He contradicts what those other religions teach about him and what they think *religion* is all about. In Scripture Jesus proclaims boldly, "I am the way and the truth and the life. No one comes to the Father *except* through me" (John 14:6; emphasis added). Peter so simply stated the same thought, "Salvation is found in no one else, for there is no other name under heaven given to men by which we must be saved" (Acts 4:12).

Claiming that God has revealed himself in many different ways by many different names is a belief fostered more to keep outward earthly peace than to convey heavenly spiritual truth. The only saving revelation of God is that which comes through Jesus Christ and proclaims not human morality but God's own perfection as our salvation.

Q: How does Islam differ from Christianity?

A: The Islamic faith believes that there is only one God, whom Muslims call Allah, but it rejects the teaching of the Trinity. Muslims revere Jesus highly as one of the greatest prophets of Allah, even teaching the virgin birth, but they refuse to believe that Jesus was both God and man. In addition, the Islamic faith teaches that sinners make up for their own sins by showing Allah their obedience. One Islamic author puts it this way: "The idea of a vicarious sacrifice [one person offering himself in the place of another] is therefore alien to Islam, and the claim that Jesus, or anyone else, had to be slain in atonement for human sins is unacceptable. God's forgiveness, in Islam, is to be sought through sincere repentance and doing righteousness" (Hassan Hathout, *Reading the Muslim Mind*, page 33). The difference between Islam and Christianity is the difference between a religion of earning forgiveness and a religion of receiving God's gift of forgiveness through Jesus Christ.

 What about those who claim to worship the God of the Bible but who do not believe that Jesus is fully God from all eternity, like members of the Church of Jesus Christ of Latter-day Saints (Mormons) or Jehovah's Witnesses?

The apostle John wrote in his second epistle, "Many deceivers, who do not acknowledge Jesus Christ as coming in the flesh, have gone out into the world" (2 John 7). All who refuse to acknowledge that the one who came "in the flesh" is God himself are deceivers who do not know God and who do nothing but deceive and confuse others. Despite all their talk about the God of the Bible, Mormons and Jehovah's Witnesses do not know God as he has clearly revealed himself in the Bible. Such deceivers may be very sincere in what they share, but their sincerity and devotion does not change the fact that what they share is spiritual deception.

Why is knowledge of "Jesus Christ as coming in the flesh" so important? If the one who bled and died on the cross was not the eternal Son of God, then we are still in our sins and under God's judgment. The Scriptures remind us, "No man can redeem the life of another or give to God a ransom for him" (Psalm 49:7). Only the God-man Savior could make us right with God. We needed a Savior who was "in the flesh," a true human being like us, so that he could place himself under the law's perfect demands that we had broken. He had to be human to suffer and die in our place. At the same time, he had to be God so that his perfect life and innocent death would count as the perfect substitution for all who have ever lived.

Q: Since people of the Jewish faith worship the God of the Old Testament, why don't they believe in the same God?

A: God chose Israel as the nation from which he would bring into the world the Savior, through whom "all peoples on earth [would] be blessed" (Genesis 12:3). The Old Testament tells the interesting and important story of the Israelites. When the Savior came, he was a Jew as God promised, but sadly, "his own did not receive him" (John 1:11). The first Christians were almost all Jews, yet many of their own people rejected Jesus. By that rejection of the world's true and only Messiah, they ceased being worshipers of the true God. Those who today profess the Jewish faith do not know the true God because they continue to reject Jesus as the Messiah. He is the one eternal Son of God who took on flesh and blood. Only those who by the power of the Spirit know and confess Jesus Christ as their Savior truly have the right to the name "children of God" (John 1:12). Of course, it is from all nations that God seeks to win his children, including those who are Jewish.

2. We believe that God has revealed himself in nature. "The heavens declare the glory of God; the skies proclaim the work of his hands" (Psalm 19:1). "Since the creation of the world God's invisible qualities—his eternal power and divine nature—have been clearly seen, being understood from what has been made, so that men are without excuse" (Romans 1:20). So there is no excuse for atheists. Since the requirements of the law are written on people's hearts, the consciences of people also bear witness that there is a God to whom they are accountable (Romans 2:15). However, nature and conscience present only a partial revelation of God and one that is not able to show the way to heaven.

Q: What does it mean that God has "revealed himself"?

A: The word *revelation* means "to make something known that otherwise would remain unknown." God desires that we know who he is, believe in him, and enjoy fellowship with him as his children now and forever. In order for these things to happen, God is determined to "reveal" himself to the world he has created. He does not want humanity to be ignorant of who he is and what he has done.

God tells us how he does this. First, he has given all humans what we call the natural knowledge of God. This means that we can know something about God by observing the wonders of what he has created and by listening to the voice of conscience that he planted within each of us. Through created things and our consciences, God simply seeks to convince every human being that he exists.

This natural knowledge of God is not enough. Neither the beauty and power of nature nor the voices of our consciences will lead us to an accurate and saving knowledge of God. As the apostle Paul tells us in 1 Corinthians, "No eye has seen, no ear has heard, no mind has conceived what God has prepared for those who love him" (2:9). God wants to make sure that we know exactly who he is and what he has done for us, so God has also revealed to us who he is in a second way. This second way we often call the revealed knowledge of God. This is the knowledge that God has given us in the Bible. It is through this revealed knowledge of God that we can come to know not just that some "god" must exist but who the true God is. This revealed knowledge of God also teaches us the wonderful truth of the eternal heaven he has prepared for us in Jesus.

Q: Why is God's revelation of himself in nature and our consciences not able to show someone the way to heaven?

A: We can learn much about God from observing the wonders of his creation. The majesty, beauty, and wonder of his creation teaches us that God is wise, loving, and powerful (Romans 1:20). From the testimony of our consciences—as they commend us for doing right but condemn us when we sin—we learn that God is holy and that sin deserves his judgment (Romans 2:14,15).

But while such knowledge about God is important, it leaves large gaps in our knowledge of God. While nature and our consciences both powerfully witness to the existence of a "god," they can never teach us to know exactly who he is. Our consciences can show us our guilt and teach us that we are subject to God's judgment, but our consciences could never know about the death and resurrection of Jesus Christ. That information must come from what God tells us—it must be revealed to us—or we would never know. That is why we thank our gracious God that he has given us far more than what we can know from nature and our consciences.

The apostle Paul tells us in Acts 17 that God gave evidence of himself in nature and our consciences so that "men would seek him and perhaps reach out for him and find him" (verse 27). However, humans stubbornly either ignored the truth found in nature and their consciences or they invented their own gods. As Paul tells us, "There is no one who understands, no one who seeks God" (Romans 3:11). Humans are responsible for their refusal to listen to nature and their consciences. They are "without excuse" (Romans 1:20).

Since many live without the gospel, we who know Jesus have a powerful reminder to proclaim the message of God's revealed law and gospel. Our prayer is that the many who are now living in ignorance of God's truth may be brought to repentance and faith.

3. We believe that God has given the full revelation of himself in his Son, the Lord Jesus Christ. "No one has ever seen God, but God the One and Only, who is at the Father's side, has made him known" (John 1:18). In Jesus, God has revealed himself as the Savior-God, who "so loved the world that he gave his one and only Son, that whoever believes in him shall not perish but have eternal life" (John 3:16).

Q: How can Scripture say, "No one has ever seen God" when Jesus appeared on earth to give us the "full revelation" of God?

A: Jesus reminds us that "God is spirit" (John 4:24). Except for Jesus, God is not flesh and blood as we are. The apostle Paul also reminds us that God is the one "who alone is immortal and who lives in unapproachable light, whom no one has seen or can see" (1 Timothy 6:16). Although God has at times given glimpses of his glory to human beings (consider Moses seeing God's "back" in Exodus 33 and 34), no one this side of heaven has ever seen God in his full, unveiled majesty.

That is true; it was true even when Jesus took on our flesh and blood. Jesus has possessed all divine majesty from eternity, yet he humbled himself during his earthly ministry. In Philippians 2:7, Paul reminds us that Jesus took "the form of a servant" (from the NIV footnote, which is a better translation). It is no wonder then that one of the greatest joys of heaven will be to see God "as he is" (1 John 3:2).

Q: How can we be confident that the Bible is true if other religions claim that their holy books are also true?

A: It is true that almost every religion possesses its own holy book. There are the Koran of Islam, the *Bhagavad Gita* of Hinduism, and the *Book of Mormon* of The Church of Jesus Christ of Latter-day Saints, just to name a few. All of these books claim to reveal truth about spiritual things. Except for the Bible, the basic message of these books is always the same. They tell us that we can gain the love and blessing of God by what we do. In eastern religions, holy books hold out escapes from the physical world through devotion and meditation.

But the Bible tells a different message. First of all, only the Bible tells us that God's love and blessings are gifts of God. They come to us through what Jesus did while he was on earth. Salvation is not based on what we must do but on what God himself has done in our place. That is a strong indication that the origin of our holy book is different from the rest.

There is a second difference in the holy books of the world. We can illustrate it best by a well-known verse from the Christmas story in Luke 2. "In those days Caesar Augustus issued a decree that a census should be taken of the entire Roman world. (This was the first census that took place while Quirinius was governor of Syria.)" (verses 1,2). Other holy books of the world tend to deal with nothing but unprovable opinion about spiritual matters. The Bible, on the other hand, is unafraid to speak of real historical events that match with documented history. There actually was a Roman emperor named Augustus, a governor of Syria named Quirinius, and a census in the Roman world at the time of Christ's birth. The Bible is not afraid that it will be proved wrong because it is the revealed truth of the God of all history. It is not something spun out of the imagination of a human mind.

Third, consider the amazing detail of clearly fulfilled prophecy. Psalm 22 and Isaiah 53 were written centuries before their fulfillment, which is recorded in Matthew, Mark,

Luke, and John. The Bible's accuracy of specific prophecy and specific fulfillment is unparalleled among the holy books of the world.

Finally, Scripture makes its own claims of what it is. "Above all, you must understand that no prophecy of Scripture came about by the prophet's own interpretation. For prophecy never had its origin in the will of man, but men spoke from God as they were carried along by the Holy Spirit" (2 Peter 1:20,21). Every word of Scripture is the "living and active" (Hebrews 4:12) testimony of the Holy Spirit himself. The best proof of that is simply to read the Bible and experience firsthand its powerful truth. The Bible is its own best defender when it works its wonders on our hearts as we read it and take it to heart.

4. We believe that God has also given a written revelation for all people in the Holy Scriptures. His revelation in the Bible has two main messages, the law and the gospel. The law declares what is right and wrong, and it threatens God's punishment for sin. The gospel presents the love of God, which he has shown especially by providing salvation from sin through Jesus Christ.

Q: ▪ Where in the Bible do we find the distinction ▪ between law and gospel?

A: ▪ The entire Bible constantly holds these two main teachings before us. The twin messages of the law and gospel, that is, the law declaring the perfection God demands of us and the gospel proclaiming the message of what God freely gives to us in Jesus, are found everywhere in the Scriptures. Perhaps the place to see the distinction between the two most plainly is in the first three chapters of Paul's letter to the Christians in Rome. After the letter's introduction and Paul's announcement of his basic theme (1:17), Paul launches into a heart-piercing call to repentance directed at both Jews and Gentiles. From 1:18 through 3:20, Paul heralds the demands of the law so that "every mouth may be silenced and the whole world held accountable to God" (3:19). That is precisely the chief purpose of the law—to rob us of any hope of saving ourselves.

Beginning with Romans 3:21, Paul gives us one of the fullest expositions of the gospel that can be found in the Scriptures. To hearts crushed by the law and overcome by sin and guilt, Paul wrote, "A righteousness from God, apart from law, has been made known, to which the Law and the Prophets [that is, the whole Old Testament Scriptures] testify. This righteousness from God comes through faith in Jesus Christ to all who believe" (3:21,22). These sections of Romans hold before us the clearest and simplest distinction between the law and the gospel.

Q: Why is it so important for every Christian to be able to distinguish between law and gospel?

A: If we fail to understand that the demands of the law are impossible to keep, every proud human heart will always want to claim some human moral value or virtue instead of clinging completely to the cross of Christ. If we fail to see the complete and perfect sacrifice of Christ as God's total answer to human sin and imperfection, we claim that we deserve salvation. Then we may be led to despair by consciences that know our sins all too well. A proper understanding of law and gospel guards us from Satan's two basic temptations: pride and despair.

5. We believe that the entire Bible is Christ-centered. In the Old Testament God repeatedly promised a divine deliverer from sin, death, and hell. The New Testament proclaims that this promised deliverer has come in the person of Jesus of Nazareth. Jesus himself says of the Old Testament, "These are the Scriptures that testify about me" (John 5:39).

Q: **How could believers in Old Testament times be saved by faith in Jesus if Christ had not yet lived or died as the Savior?**

A: God in his faithfulness never fails to keep a single promise. Therefore, once God had promised to Adam and Eve that an "offspring" of the woman would "crush [the serpent's] head" (Genesis 3:15), it was as good as done. God's promise was true even though several thousand years of world history intervened between the Garden of Eden and the hill called Calvary. The sins committed before Christ came to earth were charged to his account just as were the sins committed after he came. In God's sight, faith in the Savior who would live, die, and rise again is no different from faith in the Savior who did live, die, and rise again. Paul made that same point when he wrote, "God presented him [Jesus] as a sacrifice of atonement, through faith in his blood. He did this to demonstrate his justice, because in his forbearance he had left the sins committed beforehand unpunished—he did it to demonstrate his justice at the present time, so as to be just and the one who justifies those who have faith in Jesus" (Romans 3:25,26).

Q: **What are some key portions of the Old Testament that show that the whole Bible is centered on Christ?**

A: The most obvious Christ-centered portions of the Old Testament are the numerous sections of prophecy about the Messiah. The book of Isaiah alone is filled with examples of such messianic prophecies. Look, for example, at chapters 7, 9, 11, 40, 42, 50, 52, and 53. But in addition to the more obvious sections of the Old Testament that proclaim Christ, consider also all the sin offerings of the Old Testament in which animals died as substitutes for the people who committed the sins. In every one of those sacrifices, God gave a picture of what was to come in the one who would offer himself as the great substitute for the sins of the world. As the author to the Hebrews wrote, "Day after day every priest stands and performs his religious duties; again and again he offers the same sacrifices, which can never take away sins. But when this priest [Jesus Christ] had offered for all time one sacrifice for sins, he sat down at the right hand of God" (10:11,12). Our problem is not that we see Christ too often on the pages of the Old Testament. It is that we do not see him often enough.

6. We believe that God gave the Scriptures through men whom he chose, using the language they knew and the style of writing they had. He used Moses and the prophets to write the Old Testament in Hebrew (some portions in Aramaic) and the evangelists and apostles to write the New Testament in Greek.

Q: What is the Aramaic language, and what portions of the Bible are written in that language?

A: Aramaic, like Hebrew, is a Semitic language. The two languages are very closely related and use the same alphabet. Aramaic became the common language for God's Old Testament people from the time of the Babylonian captivity (about 600 B.C.) and was the language spoken by the common people of Jesus' time. While Hebrew is the predominant language in which God inspired the Old Testament, there are a few sections of the Old Testament that were written in Aramaic. Two words in Genesis 31:47; Ezra 4:8–6:18 and 7:12-26; Jeremiah 10:11; and Daniel 2:4–7:28 were written in the Aramaic language.

Q: Why did God use the Greek language for the New Testament?

A: Since God nowhere in Scripture tells us his exact reason for using the Greek language, we can only offer some best-guess observations from history. By doing this we may only be scratching the surface of the many reasons why God, in his perfect wisdom, used Greek as the original language of the New Testament.

The conquests of Alexander the Great (fourth century B.C.) helped spread the Greek language throughout much of the ancient world. Shortly after Alexander, Greek became the language of commerce and business in the Roman Empire. It seems to have enjoyed even more of an international status than English does today. Those who received any formal education often were familiar with Greek in addition to their own native tongues. Therefore, the inspired words of the New Testament were familiar without the need of translation to many people in much of the inhabited world. In addition, Greek has a rich vocabulary and is known for its attention to grammatical detail. These two factors made Greek especially suitable for passing on the depth of meaning that God wished to communicate in his revelation to us.

Q: **Since there were many other books written in both Old and New Testament times that claimed to be written by inspired prophets or apostles, how do we know that we have the right books in the Bible?**

A: The accepted books of both the Old Testament and New Testament are often called the canon. But the Christian church did not create this canon. Instead God's people over time came to recognize which books are genuine and belong in the Scriptures.

It is true that many other books with claims of being authentic books of Scripture were written in both Old and New Testament times, but they were rejected as something less than God's inspired words. Those books are commonly referred to as Old and New Testament *apocrypha*, or pseudepigrapha (false writings).

Let's consider the canon of the Old Testament first. At the time of Jesus, the Old Testament as we know it had already been gathered and received as God's inspired Word. The beginning of the gathering of the Old Testament canon is recorded in Scripture itself as Moses commanded those in charge of the ark of the covenant to place his five inspired books beside the ark (Deuteronomy 31:26). By the time of Jesus' earthly ministry, all the inspired books of the Old Testament that we know today were included in the accepted canon of Israel. Nowhere did Jesus speak a word against the books that his Old Testament people had gathered and that all revered as inspired by God. Far from making any suggested additions or subtractions, he even spoke of that canon as the complete revelation about himself in Old Testament times.

For instance, when talking with his disciples the first Easter evening, he said, "Everything must be fulfilled that is written about me in the Law of Moses, the Prophets and the Psalms" (Luke 24:44). Jesus used the common three-part name for the Old Testament that was in use in his day: "Law of Moses, the Prophets and the Psalms." He spoke of them all as fully faithful portions of God's revelation. Clearly if God's people had included unauthentic books among their list of inspired books or if they had failed to include books that were inspired, Jesus would not have spoken in such an approving tone of their accepted canon.

We do not have the words of Jesus himself to guide us in the gathering of the New Testament canon, yet evidence within the New Testament Scriptures suggests the beginning of this gathering of books. Peter wrote in his second epistle, "Bear in mind that our Lord's patience means salvation, just as our dear brother Paul also wrote you with the wisdom that God gave him. He writes the same way in all his letters, speaking in them of these matters. His letters contain some things that are hard to understand, which ignorant and unstable people distort, as they do the other Scriptures, to their own destruction" (2 Peter 3:15,16). Peter's fascinating reference reveals that already while Peter was still alive the letters of Paul were gathered and recognized as inspired portions of Holy Scripture.

The books of the New Testament come from the first generation of Christians—those who lived at the time of Jesus. Our faith is founded on the teaching of the apostles themselves. The long life of the apostle John also helps verify the list of books in the New Testament canon. John lived to about A.D. 100 and was a reliable witness to the authenticity of any letters that claimed to be inspired apostolic writings.

However, the most powerful witness to the authenticity of the New Testament books is the power of their witness itself. Authentic, inspired Scripture needs no one to come to its defense. The words of God are "living and active" (Hebrews 4:12) and have the power to convince each human heart of their own truthfulness and authenticity. The story of how God's New Testament believers became convinced of which books were genuine testifies to the saving power of God's inspired Word. The Holy Spirit moved the hearts of many to treasure the genuine Scriptures, collect them, copy them, and share them. We conclude that God did not desire for his inspired Word to be lost in the dusty corners of history.

7. We believe that in a miraculous way that goes beyond all human investigation, God the Holy Spirit moved these men to write his Word. These men "spoke from God as they were carried along by the Holy Spirit" (2 Peter 1:21). What they said was spoken "not in words taught us by human wisdom but in words taught by the Spirit" (1 Corinthians 2:13). Every thought they expressed and every word they used were given them by the Holy Spirit. Saint Paul wrote to Timothy, "All Scripture is God-breathed" (2 Timothy 3:16). The church has called this miraculous process *inspiration,* which means "breathing into." Since every word of Scripture was inspired, we also call this process verbal inspiration, or word-for-word inspiration. This is not to be equated with mechanical dictation, since the Holy Spirit guided the writers as they used their individual vocabularies and writing styles.

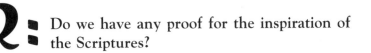 Do we have any proof for the inspiration of the Scriptures?

A: While the Scripture references listed in this paragraph from *This We Believe* state explicitly that God gave the authors of Scripture every word they were to write, perhaps the most powerful proof of Scripture's inspiration is the testimony the Spirit gives whenever the Scriptures are read. The Holy Spirit is always at work in the hearts of those who hear the message of the Bible. We can also add that the perfect fulfillment of all biblical prophecy is a further evidence of the divine inspiration of the Scriptures.

Q: Is it unreasonable to say that the inspired Scriptures testify to their own inspiration?

A: Scripture cannot be faulted for stating a simple fact, even if that fact is about its own reliability. God is the highest witness of all, and the Word is his witness about himself. For Scripture to have remained silent on the point of its own inspiration could have easily been regarded as an argument against its inspiration.

Remember that those who read the Bible find that its most powerful witness to the truth of inspiration comes from the power it possesses to convict hearts. This power is not limited to our own age, but the power of the Bible stretches back in history to the words Moses first wrote. God's Word has demonstrated a power on human hearts throughout history. The Bible is self-authenticating and proves its inspiration by the power of its message.

Q: Why doesn't belief in an inspired and errorless Bible make us worshipers of a book instead of a Savior?

A: How do we know who Jesus is? How can we know what Jesus has done for us? Where do we look to find what his life and death mean for us? Without the revelation of who Jesus is, what he has done for us, and what that means for us, we would remain ignorant of Jesus and his salvation. What John tells us near the end of his gospel is a fitting purpose statement for all of Scripture: "These are written that you may believe that Jesus is the Christ, the Son of God, and that by believing you may have life in his name" (John 20:31). The Bible and Jesus are not competing for the loyalty of our hearts. Rather, an inspired and errorless Bible gives us faithful and reliable information about the Savior in whom we believe. While we can logically divide Jesus from the revelation that shares him with us, practically speaking, the two always go together.

Q: How can we say there is no possibility of errors in the inspired texts when there was a human element involved in the process of inspiration?

A: Human beings make mistakes. But human beings under inspiration by the Holy Spirit do not record mistakes. In his great love and power, God saw to it that by the miracle of his Son's incarnation, life, death, and resurrection we were purchased from sin, death, and hell. That same God by his love and power worked the miracle of inspiration to provide us a faithful and absolutely reliable testimony to that salvation. The writers were human. But the intelligence or reputation of each of the inspired writers does not guarantee reliability. The perfect wisdom of the Holy Spirit is that guarantee. That is why Jesus can make the simple and yet profound statement that "The Scripture cannot be broken" (John 10:35).

8. We believe that Scripture is a unified whole, true and without error in everything it says, for the Savior said, "The Scripture cannot be broken" (John 10:35). Therefore it is the infallible authority and guide for everything we believe and do.

Q: How can we sinful human beings claim to possess absolute truth?

A: Absolute truth exists because what God has revealed will always be faithful and true. This gift of truth does not depend on sinful human beings. We do not create this truth, but God has revealed it through the inspired Scriptures. Even if every human being in the world refused to believe every single thing God has said, God's message would remain true in every part. Jesus prayed, "Sanctify them by the truth; your word is truth" (John 17:17). There is such a thing as absolute, unchanging, and unchangeable truth because "God is not a man, that he should lie, nor a son of man, that he should change his mind" (Numbers 23:19).

Q: How can a book whose most recent portion was written almost two thousand years ago still speak the truth today to our rapidly changing culture?

A: While many outward things change from age to age—clothing, transportation methods, communication tools—in a very real sense what Solomon said in Ecclesiastes 1:9 still remains true: "There is nothing new under the sun." Human beings still have a basic problem. Simply, we are creatures isolated from our Creator because of our sinful nature.

We neither trust in him nor love him above all things. When we are born, we lack a love for our Creator. In addition, we do not by nature love our neighbors as ourselves. Our lovelessness toward God and our neighbors is still the root cause behind all the trouble and grief of this world. These basic problems with God and our neighbors don't change just because our chariots are now powered by engines or because our letters are now sent by electricity.

In spite of all the advances in many fields, we still are unable to change one reality. Life here on earth is temporary. We will all die at some point, and that cannot be changed, even by great advances in medical science.

And there's something else that will never change. The only answer to all that troubles us is found in him who, as our substitute, loved God and our neighbors perfectly in our place, died under the curse for our sins, and rose to proclaim that our rescue was complete. In Jesus we find forgiveness for all that troubles us, new power to love God and our neighbors, and a sure hope of victory over death itself. The Bible will always remain perfectly relevant in every age because it reveals both our unchanging basic needs and, in Jesus, the answer to those needs.

9. We believe that the Bible is fully sufficient, clearly teaching people all they need to know to get to heaven. It makes them "wise for salvation through faith in Christ Jesus" (2 Timothy 3:15), and it equips them for "every good work" (2 Timothy 3:17). Since God's plan of salvation has been fully revealed in the canonical books of the Bible, we need and expect no other revelations (Hebrews 1:1,2). The church is built on the teachings of the apostles and prophets (Ephesians 2:20).

Q:

Since the Bible is "fully sufficient," does that mean that there can never be further revelations by God?

A: The Scriptures do not promise that there will be further general revelations for all people or specific revelations for individuals.

When it comes to general revelations for all people, Scripture gives strong indication that in the Old and New Testaments we possess all that God has planned to reveal to us. As Paul tells Timothy, "From infancy you have known the holy Scriptures, which are able to make you wise for salvation through faith in Christ Jesus. All Scripture is God-breathed and is useful for teaching, rebuking, correcting and training in righteousness, so that the man of God may be thoroughly equipped for every good work" (2 Timothy 3:15-17). In the Old and New Testament Scriptures, we possess all we need to know to be "wise for salvation" and all the knowledge and strength we need "for every good work."

The book of Hebrews begins, "In the past God spoke to our forefathers through the prophets at many times and in various ways, but in these last days he has spoken to us by his Son, whom he appointed heir of all things, and through whom he made the universe" (Hebrews 1:1,2). Notice how the inspired author contrasts God's Old Testament revelation with his New Testament revelation. The author speaks of the Old Testament "in the past" and the New Testament revelation of the Son coming in "these last days." God spoke in preparation for his Son's life and work (Old Testament), and God spoke of that work while it was in progress and when it was completed (New Testament). We do not await further word from God but only the final fulfillment on the very last day of all he has already promised us. As those who live in the continuation of the "last days," we need nothing more from God. With Isaiah, we need to encourage all people to turn "to the law and to the testimony! If they do not speak according to this word, they have no light of dawn" (Isaiah 8:20).

We believe that the Scripture of the Old and New Testaments is God's sufficient revelation. At the same time, the Scripture provides a way to test the words of those who claim to have received further revelation from God. Many have claimed to have special revelations from God that are in addition to the Bible. Any revelation that claims to be from God but contradicts what the Old and New Testament Scriptures say clearly marks itself as the work of man, not God. God will never contradict himself.

Some also claim that God has given them visions, dreams, or revelations about specific events or decisions in their lives. But God has not promised such revelations or dreams, and we have no promise from God that they are reliable. God simply asks us to trust in the truth that he has revealed in the Bible and directs us to put its principles into action in our lives.

While God does not promise that his children will receive such specific revelations, such specific revelations cannot be categorically ruled out. Every supposed revelation would have to be compared with what is already known in Scripture. Anything that contradicts the Scriptures could not possibly come from God.

The danger in looking for such special revelations is that those waiting for such visions or dreams ignore the very real answers God has already given in his Word. The means of grace, which is the gospel in Word and sacrament, are neglected for that which seems more spectacular and for that which caters to our own spiritual appetites. While God has not asked us to be the judges of the reality and validity of all such revelations, he does urge us to continue to direct people to the sure and certain revelation that we have in the means of grace. There alone we have what God has promised to use to create and strengthen faith.

Q: If Scripture "clearly" teaches all we need to know to get to heaven, then why are there so many different interpretations about what Scripture teaches?

A: Has God made these interpretations? Where did they come from? The blame for all the different interpretations cannot be leveled at God, as if he gave us such a hopelessly confusing and mysterious revelation that no one can truly know what it says. If that were true, God would not be perfectly wise. He would be the author of confusion, not truth.

Instead, differences in interpretation arise chiefly from two problems in the human heart. First, human beings insist on believing only what is reasonable to them. Humans often let reason judge Scripture, thereby refusing to acknowledge that God's reason is far above ours (Isaiah 55:8,9). Exalting human reason leads to a distortion of the Word. Often the message of the Scripture is twisted to make it more acceptable to our way of thinking. Paul reminds us that the "things that come from the Spirit of God . . . are foolishness" (1 Corinthians 2:14) to natural man.

Second, humans possess a sinful pride. Our naturally proud hearts do not like to be confronted with our sinfulness or to be told that the only way for us to be acceptable before God is through the life, death, and resurrection of Jesus Christ. As Paul warned Timothy, "The time will come when men will not put up with sound doctrine. Instead, to suit their own desires, they will gather around them a great number of teachers to say what their itching ears want to hear" (2 Timothy 4:3). Human beings by nature are inclined toward what they "want to hear" rather than what they need to hear. That is why human pride is forever fighting against the saving message of salvation by grace alone through faith alone. Instead of trusting only in Christ, humans attempt to add something to Christ's completed work—perhaps some good works, some decision to believe, or some noble intentions. But the gospel leaves no room for any human pride or boasting.

Q: **What is meant by "the canonical books of the Bible"?**

A: "The canonical books of the Bible" are those books of the Old Testament (39 books) and New Testament (27 books) that the church has learned to recognize as verbally inspired by God. The church did not create the canon but rather came to recognize the uniqueness of the books that the Spirit had given to the church. Please see the questions and answers under paragraph 6 for a fuller description of the canon.

10. We believe and accept the Bible on its own terms, accepting as factual history what it presents as history and recognizing as figurative speech what is evident as such. We believe that Scripture must interpret Scripture, clear passages throwing light on those less easily understood. We believe that no authority—whether it is human reason, science, or scholarship—may stand in judgment over Scripture. Sound scholarship will faithfully search out the true meaning of Scripture without presuming to pass judgment on it.

Q: **How are we to know when to read the Bible as factual history and when to read it as figures of speech?**

A: The principle of scriptural interpretation, "Scripture interprets Scripture," is the key to this question. Scripture itself will indicate when it intends us to see figures of speech. For example, Jesus most often clearly marks the beginning of his parables by saying, "The kingdom of heaven is like . . ." (Matthew 13:24). In other cases, a careful reading of the surrounding context of the chapter or, at times, the whole book will often make it clear whether the Scripture is talking of factual history or is using a figure of speech to make a point. Another good rule of thumb is to assume that Scripture is speaking literally unless there is clear indication in the context to the contrary.

Q: **How have human reason and science stood in judgment of Scripture?**

A: Human reason considers many teachings of the gospel to be foolishness, such as the virgin birth of Christ, his bodily resurrection from the grave, and the idea that he was fully eternal God and fully man in one person. The example of the teaching of evolution reveals unbelieving bias against God's answer to human origins. Evolution assumes that God, if he exists, cannot directly affect human history. Therefore, a miraculous creation and the effects of a worldwide flood are rejected as impossible.

Q: **How can we say that no authority may stand in judgment over Scripture and still honor the Fourth Commandment by obeying people in authority over us?**

 A: Since the Scriptures themselves command us to give obedience to parents and to other divinely instituted authorities, such as the government (see Romans 13), there is no contradiction. Of course, if those authorities would command us to do something Scripture forbids or would insist that we omit something Scripture commands, then we would need to follow the example of the apostles who told the Jewish Sanhedrin, "We must obey God rather than men!" (Acts 5:29).

11. We believe that the original Hebrew text of the Old Testament and the Greek text of the New Testament are the inspired Word of God. Translations of the Hebrew and Greek that accurately reflect the meaning of the original text convey God's truth to people and can properly be called the Word of God.

Q: Since the Bible was written in Hebrew and Greek and not in English, why can we call our English translations the Word of God when they are not in the original languages?

A: While God did inspire the Scriptures in the Hebrew and Greek languages, the Word of God is not limited to the sounds of the syllables in the original language. The Word of God is the meaning of the message of those inspired words. When a translation is faithful to the meaning of the original Hebrew and Greek, then what it shares is the Word of God— no less than the meaning expressed in the Hebrew and Greek.

Q: Is someone who doesn't know Greek or Hebrew at a disadvantage when it comes to knowing God's revelation?

A: There is no language test at the gates of heaven, and God's saving truth translates beautifully into every language humans speak. However, there is no doubt that knowledge of Greek and Hebrew is of great value. First, while there are many good English translations that can be used with a high degree of confidence, those who know Hebrew and Greek will be able to tell when a Bible translation has missed the precise meaning found in those original languages. Second, even when the translation has been faithful to the meaning of the original, there are still many times when a beautiful word picture or an important point of grammar from the original language cannot be expressed without excessive wordiness in the English translations. While the meaning found in the translation will be the same, the word picture or point of grammar that would have helped the reader more fully grasp the beauty of the message may have been lost.

For these two reasons alone, it is vital that those who prepare for the pastoral ministry be thoroughly trained in the original languages. That allows them with an extra measure of confidence to stand up and say, "This is what the Lord says!"

12. Although the original documents themselves have been lost, we believe that the Lord in his providential care has accurately preserved the Hebrew and Greek texts through the many hand-copied manuscripts that exist. Although there are minor differences or "variants" between the various hand-copied manuscripts, these variants do not cause any changes in doctrine.

Q: Why did God allow the original documents to be lost?

A: Since Scripture makes no mention of this, all we can offer is an unauthoritative guess. Some call the original documents the *autographs*. They are the actual manuscripts on which the inspired authors wrote their letters. God may have allowed all of those *autographs* to disappear so that the pieces of paper would not be revered more than the message they contained. Yet God's reasons may be many and far wiser than this guess.

It is more important to marvel at the great care with which thousands of handwritten copies of both testaments were preserved for us. We can thank God for the marvelous way he saw to it that both his Old and New Testament churches faithfully preserved thousands of copies of their original manuscripts. Even though all the copies are not identical, the quantity and quality of the many different manuscripts of the Bible leave no doubt about what was written on the original documents by the inspired authors. God carefully preserved the truth by moving many faithful believers to copy the sacred Scriptures.

Q: Since human copyists did make mistakes, how can we be sure that what we have is the Word of God?

A: Every copyist valued the Scriptures highly and copied them with great care and accuracy. But copying the Scripture by hand was tiring and tedious work, which naturally allowed for small *variants* to creep into manuscripts. If all we had was one copy—and copies made from it—of both the Old and New Testaments, we would be at the mercy of the accuracy of that one copyist. But that's not the case. We have thousands of manuscripts from many different areas of the Christian world. Carefully comparing and studying these numerous manuscripts makes the wording of the original document clear. Even when some of the manuscript copies show a different or variant reading, we can be confident of the original. In the rare cases where we cannot be sure what the original said, we can say clearly that no teaching of the Scriptures rests in those passages.

Q: ■ How much of the Bible is affected by the variants that are mentioned?

A: ■ For the vast majority of the words of Scripture, the text is unquestioned. Only a small percentage needs to be carefully studied where different manuscripts show variant readings. What is more, the overwhelming majority of such variant readings have no effect on the obvious meanings of the verses. For instance, one of the most common variants found in the manuscripts is the variant between a first (we) or second person (you) pronoun. In Greek, several common forms of those pronouns differ by only one slight stroke of the pen. Another of the most common variants is whether a verse has just the name "Christ" or also "Jesus" along with it. It can be said with confidence that no doctrine of Scripture is in question because of variant readings.

13. We believe that the three ecumenical creeds (the Apostles', the Nicene, and the Athanasian) as well as the Lutheran Confessions as contained in the Book of Concord of 1580 express the true doctrine of Scripture. Since the doctrines they confess are drawn from Scripture alone, we are bound to them in our faith and life. Therefore all preaching and teaching in our churches and schools must be in harmony with these confessions, and we reject all the errors that they reject.

Q: Why are the Apostles', the Nicene, and the Athanasian creeds labeled "the three ecumenical creeds"?

A: While many of our Lutheran confessions (such as Luther's catechisms, the Augsburg Confession, and the Formula of Concord) are the unique possession of the Lutheran church, the Apostles', the Nicene, and the Athanasian creeds are labeled "ecumenical" because they are widely accepted in the visible Christian church across many denominational boundaries.

Q: What is the *Book of Concord?*

A: The *Book of Concord* is the official collection of all the historic confessions of faith that explain in great detail the teachings of our Lutheran church. There are six confessions of faith unique to our Lutheran church within the *Book of Concord.* These six are the Small and Large Catechism, the Augsburg Confession, the Apology (Explanation or Defense) of the Augsburg Confession, the Smalcald Articles, and the Formula of Concord.

Q: Why do we need creeds and confessions if the Bible is fully sufficient for our faith?

A: Two reasons explain why creeds and confessions have sprung up repeatedly in the history of the church. First, the very nature of faith wants to express itself. Believers want to tell others what they believe. The Apostles' Creed grew from that desire to confess what the apostles taught.

"For it is with your heart that you believe and are justified, and it is with your mouth that you confess and are saved" (Romans 10:10).

Second, false teachings and false teachers who claim scriptural support for their errors continually arise in the church. These errors have led Christians throughout the centuries to compose summaries of what they were convinced Scripture really said. Both the Nicene and Athanasian creeds came about because of false teachings that circulated in the early church. To remain silent when error tries to distort the truth of God is to allow confusion and to endanger the faith of believers. Creeds and confessions have been one way Christians throughout the centuries have stated clearly what they are convinced is the truth of Scripture.

Q: **Do we place the ecumenical creeds and our Lutheran Confessions on the same level as Scripture?**

A: The church always runs the risk of placing the words of people on the same level as the words of God. Christians also risk only parroting the good words of our spiritual ancestors, forgetting what Scriptural truths were the base for those statements. For such worship of the words of people we must always be on our guard. We believe and teach that the Scriptures alone, never the writings of people, are the source of every doctrine.

Yet when we study the Scriptures and come to the same conclusions as those who went before us, we desire to confess the same truths as they did. Others in a previous time and place beautifully stated the truths of Scripture; we do not hesitate to confess that we preach and teach just as they did. Our subscription to their confessions makes that declaration clear.

Pledging our faithfulness to teach in accordance with the Lutheran Confessions is also a safeguard for those who will be under the care of our called workers. Those who are calling Lutheran public servants to their congregations deserve to know the theological beliefs of those who will be teaching for them. A clear and unequivocal promise to teach in accord with the Lutheran Confessions is an assurance that a congregation of believers will hear nothing preached or taught that is in violation of Scripture.

14. We reject any worship that is not directed to the triune God as revealed in the Bible. We reject the use of feminine names and pronouns for God because in Scripture God reveals himself as Father and Son. We reject the opinion that all religions lead to the same God.

Q: **What's wrong with prayers that are spoken to God but don't mention Jesus in order to avoid offending those who don't believe in him?**

A: While not every prayer will contain the name of Jesus (see the Lord's Prayer), to leave Jesus' name out of a prayer so as not to offend those who don't believe in him is a denial of Jesus. He is the eternal Son of God. As Jesus reminds us, "I am the way and the truth and the life. No one comes to the Father except through me" (John 14:6). Apart from faith in Jesus, people do not know the true God nor can they pray to him. Such an approach to prayer—leaving out Jesus' name so as not to offend others—suggests that the love for the praise of people is more important than the desire to do what is right in the eyes of God.

Q: ▪ Is it intolerant to say that all religions do not ▪ lead to the same God?

A: No. All religions don't lead to the same God, as Scripture proclaims. Listen to Jesus' own words in his prayer on Maundy Thursday evening: "Now this is eternal life: that they may know you, the only true God, and Jesus Christ, whom you have sent" (John 17:3). On the last day of this world's existence, all who have ever lived will be gathered before the judgment seat of God. Jesus of Nazareth will be the one judging the living and the dead. He is the eternal Son of God who became our brother to offer his life and death as that which alone can save us. The God who said, "Turn to me and be saved, all you ends of the earth; for I am God, and there is no other" (Isaiah 45:22), is the Father who planned our salvation, the Son who won our salvation, and the Holy Spirit who has taught us to know our salvation. To hide the truth that can save someone's soul is not tolerant but unloving.

15. We reject any thought that makes only part of Scripture God's Word or that allows for the possibility of factual error in Scripture, even in so-called nonreligious matters such as historical or geographical details. We likewise reject all views that say Scripture is merely a human record of God's revelation as he encounters mankind in history, and so is a record subject to human imperfections.

Q: ▪ Since we are not saved by the historical or ▪ geographical facts of the Scriptures, why is it ▪ so important to insist that the Bible is true and factual even in those details?

A: First, we insist on the complete reliability of Scripture because we are convinced from Scripture that it is so. "Every word of God is flawless" (Proverbs 30:5).

In addition, if we decide that we cannot trust God's own words in the lesser details of history and geography, why can we suddenly trust him in the greater matters of forgiveness and eternal life? If we accept only a portion of the Scriptures as God's Word, we arrogantly decide what God should and should not say. A god who couldn't inspire truth about dates and facts does not earn our confidence about his truthfulness in general. Satan loves nothing more than to shake our confidence in any part of Scripture, because he then can shake our confidence in all of Scripture. To put it bluntly, the lie of dividing God's words into reliable and unreliable portions came from Satan himself already in the Garden of Eden when he asked, "Did God really say . . . ?" (Genesis 3:1).

16. We reject any emphasis upon Jesus as the personal Word of God (John 1:1) that minimizes the role of the Scriptures as the written Word of God (Romans 3:2).

Q: Since we worship Jesus, the personal Word of God, and not a book, isn't he much more important to us than the written Word of God?

A: Since we do not live at a time when Jesus is conducting an earthly ministry, we have no way of knowing the personal Word of God (Jesus) apart from the written Word of God (the Bible). Those who want to separate the two often seek to do so because they are not willing to listen to all that

God has to say in the Bible. After all, Jesus himself proclaimed, "These are the Scriptures that testify about me" (John 5:39).

17. We reject every effort to reduce the confessions contained in the *Book of Concord* to historical documents that do not have binding confessional significance for the church today. We likewise reject any claim that the church is bound only to those doctrines of Scripture that are specifically addressed in these confessions.

Q: **Are the confessions of the *Book of Concord* merely historical documents?**

A: Yes, the confessions in the *Book of Concord* are historical documents, but we do not think of them as *merely* historical documents. Those who claim they are merely historical documents usually do so because they no longer agree with the truths expressed in the confessions. Their approach to the confessions as only historical documents suggests that doctrine is always developing and that we today can no longer hold to all of the truths the documents confess.

Q: **Do the Lutheran Confessions discuss every doctrine of the Bible?**

A: No. The confessions of our Lutheran church do not claim to be an exhaustive resource on every doctrine of Scripture. Most of the doctrines included in the confessions are there because of false or confusing teachings within the visible church at the time the confessions were written. No questions arose about doctrines such as creation or the inspiration of Scripture. The silence of our confessions on such doctrines does not reflect ignorance or disagreement on those doctrines. The silence instead reflects that such doctrines were almost universally accepted in the visible church at that time. We are bound to teach in accord with all the doctrines of Scripture (Matthew 28:20) whether the confessions mention them or not.

Additional Reading for This Section:

Law and Gospel: Bad News—Good News by Leroy A. Dobberstein

Trinity: One God, Three Persons by Richard D. Balge

Biblical Interpretation: The Only Right Way by David P. Kuske

Law and Gospel: Foundation of Lutheran Ministry by Robert J. Koester

Bible: God's Inspired, Inerrant Word by Brian R. Keller

Section II.
CREATION, MANKIND, AND SIN

1. We believe that the universe, the world, and the human race came into existence in the beginning when God created heaven and earth and all creatures (Genesis 1,2). Further testimony to this event is found in other passages of the Old and New Testaments (for example, Exodus 20:11; Hebrews 11:3). The creation happened in the course of six consecutive days of normal length by the power of God's almighty word.

Q: Where does Scripture indicate to us precisely how old the earth is?

A: Nowhere does Scripture give us a precise calendar date for the creation of the world. God did not inspire Scripture with the purpose of helping us to fix an exact chronological date for creation. At the same time, Scripture clearly leaves no room for the millions and billions of years that evolutionary theory suggests. Why?

First, the Bible clearly presents the days of creation as 24-hour days following one another consecutively in the span of one week. The first chapter of Genesis, as well as the rest of Scripture, does not allow for a slow process of development between lower and higher species. Second, the biblical chronologies of Genesis chapters 5, 10, and 11 bring us up to the time of Abraham (about 2000 B.C.). At that point we have recorded history from secular sources. The Bible does not leave room for any longer periods of time from Adam to Abraham. Finally, even though the Hebrew word translated in Genesis as "became the father of" does not always demand a strict one-generation interval of father and son, trying to stretch any link of those chronologies beyond several generations would clearly distort beyond recognition the common use of that term.

Q: **Why do we insist that the six days of creation were "consecutive days of normal length"? Couldn't God have made the days of creation much longer?**

A: God could have created the world in any way that pleased him. But what he *could* have done is not the question. How God *did* choose to create the world and what the Bible reveals about his choice are the questions. Genesis 1 and 2 tell us that God did all his creating work in six 24-hour days. Those six days followed one another in strict sequence—together with the seventh day—to form one calendar week as we still know it today.

Moses repeats this refrain without change: "And there was evening, and there was morning—the first [second, third, etc.] day." That phrase clearly shows us that God was using the word *day* in its meaning of "calendar day" and not in the sense of "daylight" or "era." Is this a correct understanding? Yes, because numbering is used for each of the seven days with the word *day* (first, second, etc.). Such numbering is never used with the Hebrew word for "day" except when it is recounting calendar days. Further evidence for this usage of the term *day* in Genesis 1 and 2 can be found in Exodus 20:8-11. There the Israelites used six "days" for work and the seventh "day" was set aside for rest. This exactly parallels God's creating activity at the beginning of time.

Q: Don't the fossilized forms of dinosaurs and other extinct animals prove our world is millions and billions of years old?

A: The fossilized forms found in rock do not themselves prove or disprove any theory of the earth's origins. Evolutionary scientists date fossils by the rock layers in which they are found. They assume that those layers have always formed in the same speed and manner in which we see them form today. Some call this uniformitarianism. These presuppositions or assumptions are made apart from the discoveries of the fossils, and then the discoveries are dated on the basis of the presuppositions. The past is considered to be a uniform copy of the present without divine disruption or intrusion. Most discount completely an event such as the worldwide flood at the time of Noah. But the flood certainly changed the earth and altered rock formation. Similarly, the moment the universe left the hand of God it would have had an appearance of great age. Adam and Eve were not day-old infants; sedimentary rock layers may have already been in existence; light from distant galaxies light-years away already appeared in the night sky on the evening of the day they were created.

Q: Does Scripture say anything about life on other planets or in other galaxies?

A: As we strive to answer this question, please remember the chief reason that Scripture was written. John reminded us of this reason as he brought his gospel to a conclusion: "These are written that you may believe that Jesus is the Christ, the Son of God, and that by believing you may have life in his name" (John 20:31). Paul also wrote, "From infancy you have known the holy Scriptures, which are able to make you wise for salvation through faith in Christ Jesus. All Scripture is God-breathed and is useful for teaching, rebuking, correcting and training in righteousness, so that the man of God may be thoroughly equipped for every good work" (2 Timothy 3:15-17). Scripture was not written to answer every curious question we can raise but rather to give us a saving knowledge of Jesus and to give us everything we need to live godly, productive lives. Therefore, it should not surprise us that Scripture does not seek to answer this question directly. This question does not alter our certainty of salvation or our ability to live our lives to the glory of God.

But Scripture makes some indirect assertions that seem to indicate that life on earth is a unique creation of God. First, one indication of the purpose of the rest of the universe is found in the record of its creation. "And God said, 'Let there be lights in the expanse of the sky to separate the day from the night, and let them serve as signs to mark seasons and days and years, and let them be lights in the expanse of the sky to give light on the earth'" (Genesis 1:14,15). One purpose of the universe clearly seems to be to serve earth and the humans on it. Consider, for instance, how Jesus mentions signs in the heavens (Matthew 24:29) as an indication of the end of the universe as we know it. While nowhere does Scripture teach an earth-centered physical map of the universe, it does teach that the whole universe serves earth and human beings, who were originally created in God's likeness.

Second, consider that in the good news of Jesus Christ we have a message intended for "all creation" (Mark 16:15). We would have no idea what message to proclaim to intelligent and rational creatures that inhabit different planets with different histories. Since Scripture equips us for "every good work," it seems that in having equipped us for dealing with our fellow residents of earth, it has equipped us for every situation we may encounter.

Finally, consider also that when God brings the great day of judgment upon the earth, the entire universe will be destroyed and then renewed at the same time. That's what Peter tells us in his second letter when he writes, "But the day of the Lord will come like a thief. The heavens will disappear with a roar; the elements will be destroyed by fire, and the earth and everything in it will be laid bare" (2 Peter 3:10). Since the judgment for the sins of all people will bring an end to the whole universe, God would seem to be unjust if he would judge other intelligent creatures in the universe for the sins of all people on earth.

2. We believe that the Bible presents a true, factual, and historical account of creation.

Q: Why is it so important to hold to the Bible's account of creation when it is only belief in the gospel that saves?

A: If we cannot trust God in the details of science and history, why can we trust him with the details of eternal life and salvation? To accuse God—or his inspired writers—of error or inaccuracy in any part of his revelation is to cast doubt on every part of his revelation.

While Scripture nowhere demands that it be the only educational textbook for every detail of life, what it does reveal about things such as science or history prove just as reliable as what it reveals about life and salvation. As the psalm writers put it so simply, "O LORD . . . all your words are true" (Psalm 119:159,160) and again, "The words of the LORD are flawless" (Psalm 12:6).

3. We believe that God created Adam and Eve in his own image (Genesis 1:26,27), that is, holy and righteous. Their thoughts, desires, and will were in full harmony with God (Colossians 3:10; Ephesians 4:24). They were furthermore given the capacity to "subdue" God's creation (Genesis 1:28) and the responsibility to care for it (Genesis 2:15).

Q: What does it mean that Adam and Eve were to "subdue" God's creation? It sounds like there was something imperfect or unfinished about God's creation.

A: That Adam and Eve were to "subdue" God's creation implied neither imperfection nor incompleteness in God's creation. God's own verdict on his creation was that it was "very good" (Genesis 1:31). By commanding Adam and Eve to "subdue" the earth, God gave to Adam and Eve an opportunity to use their wisdom and understanding to master the wonders of God's created order. Every legitimate discovery by a person, in the fields of technology or medicine for example, still happens as a result of God's command to "subdue" the wonders of his created world. Even if no one acknowledges God as the real author of such wonders or gives him the glory, still God has given humans a universe that is beautiful, intricate, and wonderfully made.

Q: If caring for the world is God's responsibility, why did God give humans the responsibility to care for his creation?

A: God delights to do much of his work through human agents. For example, in the spiritual realm, it is the Holy Spirit who brings us to faith through the gospel, yet God uses human agents to proclaim that gospel. Likewise, in the physical realm, God ultimately provides for and protects his creation, yet he uses human beings as agents (parents, employers, police, soldiers, etc.) to do much of his providing and protecting. To be such a tool or agent of God at work in this world is one of the greatest honors God can give to a person. We are involved in this work whenever we use the abilities and resources God gives to serve his purpose on earth. In this way, God enriches our lives—often through others—in order to pass on those gifts to even more people. The apostle Paul referred to this great chain reaction when he wrote this in 2 Corinthians 9:10,11: "Now he who supplies seed to the sower and bread for food will also supply and increase your store of seed and will enlarge the harvest of your righteousness. You will be made rich in every way so that you can be generous on every occasion, and through us your generosity will result in thanksgiving to God." Of course, only Christians recognize that every gift comes to us freely from God because of his grace to us in Christ Jesus (Romans 8:32). We then find delight in giving.

Q: **If all people come from Adam and Eve, how did all the different races of humankind come to be?**

A: The genetic code God gave Adam and Eve was so complex and miraculous that all the possibilities of all the different races existed within their genetic makeup. God has also equipped people with an amazing ability to adapt to their surroundings over the course of time. Such small adaptations over the course of many generations may also help to explain some of the differences among the races. Biblical evidence of such development of different races from a common ancestry can be seen in the Table of Nations in Genesis 10.

Any kind of bigotry or racism that considers any one race better or superior cannot use the Bible as an excuse for its sin. Such prejudice and racism violates God's message of law and gospel, which proclaims that we are all equally sinners and yet are all equally clothed with the righteousness of Christ. After all, that was Paul's point in Galatians 3 when he wrote, "You are all sons of God through faith in Christ Jesus, for all of you who were baptized into Christ have clothed yourselves with Christ. There is neither Jew nor Greek, slave nor free, male nor female, for you are all one in Christ Jesus" (verses 26-28).

4. We believe that God created a multitude of good angels. Sometime after creation, a number of these angels rebelled against God under the leadership of one of their own who is called Satan or the devil (2 Peter 2:4). Ever since, these evil angels have opposed God and God's people (1 Peter 5:8).

Q: When did God create the angels?

A: This question may fascinate us, but Scripture makes no specific reference to the time of their creation. We know, of course, that God alone is eternal, so we do know that the angels were part of God's creation. All things, visible and invisible, were created during the six days of creation. We just don't know the exact day God created them.

Q: What was God's purpose in creating angels?

A: The book of Hebrews gives us the simplest and most direct answer when the author writes, "Are not all angels ministering spirits sent to serve those who will inherit salvation?" (1:14). God's angels are his created spirit-beings, which he uses to provide care and protection for his believers.

There are many examples of the services the angels offer to God's children. In Psalm 91:11,12 we see that the care they provide shields God's children from many evils and troubles. We see that the angels help gather the souls of believers to heaven at the time of their deaths (Luke 16:22) and will help gather God's children from the four corners of the earth on judgment day (Matthew 24:31). At times the angels have fulfilled the meaning of their name by communicating important messages to believers (Luke 1:26,27). The word translated "angel" in both Hebrew and Greek literally means "messenger."

While the angels serve us, they render praise and worship to their Creator. The thunderous chorus of the angels, labeled "seraphs" in Isaiah 6, and the many songs of the angels in heaven as recorded in Revelation give ample evidence of this purpose of their existence.

Q: How long after creation did the fall of the angels take place?

A: Scripture supplies no definite time sequence for the fall of the angels. We only have two bookends between which that fall must have taken place. At the end of God's creating work on the sixth day, God pronounced everything that he had created to be "very good" (Genesis 1:31). At that time no evil existed anywhere in God's creation.

The other bookend is the temptation of Adam and Eve in the Garden of Eden. By that time the fall of the angels had obviously taken place. The devil as an evil creature tempted Adam and Eve with disobedience to God. Beyond setting up those two bookends, Scripture gives us no other details of when the angels fell.

Q: Why did Satan and so many other angels rebel against God?

A: Scripture offers no direct explanation of the fall of the angels. The closest thing Scripture offers is the hint given by Paul in 1 Timothy 3:6. There Paul speaks of the qualifications for spiritual leaders in congregations. He writes that such leaders "must not be a recent convert, or he may become conceited and fall under the same judgment as the devil." Paul lets us know that pride was behind the rebellion of the devil and his angels, but exactly how that pride spawned the rebellion of the angels is not revealed to us. We can say that any rebellion against the God of infinite love and kindness defies rational explanation. All such rebellion is arrogant foolishness. That is true both of the fall of the angels as well as the fall of Adam and Eve.

Q: **If God knows all the things that will happen, why didn't he prevent Satan and the evil angels from rebelling against him?**

A: There is much here that God has not revealed to us. But God knows all things before they happen and has unlimited power. Every day God does indeed frustrate and hinder many evil plans of the wicked. (See Psalm 2:1-6 for an example of that principle.) At times, in his perfect wisdom, he permits his creatures to do the evil that he hates. That does not change his knowledge, power, wisdom, or love. While God often has hidden purposes behind such permission, he keeps us from understanding exactly what he is doing.

We have many questions about the persistence of evil in our world, but two things we know. First, God has given us everything in Jesus. He will not withhold anything good from us (Romans 8:31,32) and will even make evil serve his people (Romans 8:28). Second, we are limited creatures of God. We simply must marvel with the apostle Paul, "Oh, the depth of the riches of the wisdom and knowledge of God! How unsearchable his judgments, and his paths beyond tracing out! Who has known the mind of the Lord? Or who has been his counselor?" (Romans 11:33,34).

Q: **How do we avoid calling God the author of evil since God created Satan knowing that he would fall?**

A: When God proclaimed that everything in creation was "very good" (Genesis 1:31), that included creating angels and human beings with the free will to choose to love and serve God. Free will remained "very good," even though it carried the possibility that both angels and humankind would abuse and destroy their God-given freedom by choosing to sin. When angels, and later humans, chose to abuse God's gift, that did not make God the author of evil. He neither desired nor decreed their sin.

Here it can be somewhat helpful to remember that there is a difference between God's knowledge of an event before it happens and God's desire, or will, for that action to happen. While God knows every action before it happens, including Satan's fall, nowhere does Scripture allow us to say that God desires such evil to take place. The following passage from James applies even to Satan's fall: "When tempted, no one should say, 'God is tempting me.' For God cannot be tempted by evil, nor does he tempt anyone; but each one is tempted when, by his own evil desire, he is dragged away and enticed" (1:13,14). God's knowledge of sinful actions before they occur does not make him the author of evil.

---

5. We believe that Adam and Eve lost their divine image when they yielded to the temptation of Satan and disobeyed God's command. This brought upon them the judgment of God: "You will surely die" (Genesis 2:17). Since that time all people are conceived and born in a sinful condition (Psalm 51:5) and are inclined only to evil (Genesis 8:21). "Flesh gives birth to flesh" (John 3:6). Since all people are by nature dead in sin and separated from God (Ephesians 2:1), they are unable to reconcile themselves to God by their own efforts and deeds.

Q: How does Scripture describe this "sinful condition" into which we are born?

A: Scripture uses many pictures to describe our "sinful condition." Two in particular help us to see clearly the sinful condition we all have at birth. In Ephesians 2:1 Paul describes it by saying, "As for you, you were dead in your transgressions and sins." As far as doing what pleases God, we are "dead" in our sins. The picture is clear: we have lost any spiritual power to do what pleases our God. To be "dead" is to be powerless.

But our "sinful condition" is actually worse than that. The second picture is also clear. While we are "dead" when it comes to pleasing God, we are not "dead" when it comes to actions against him. The Bible tells us that "the sinful mind is hostile to God" (Romans 8:7). So while we are "dead" to anything good, we are very much alive to anything that is opposed to God. That describes the two sides of the "sinful condition" that we have all inherited since the fall of Adam and Eve.

Q: If all people are totally depraved and unable to please God from birth, how do even unbelievers do so many helpful and beneficial things for others?

A: No doubt unbelievers do many helpful things that benefit their fellow human beings in this life. We call these acts of concern and kindness civic righteousness, since society in general benefits from these helpful actions of unbelievers. At the same time, we must clearly keep in mind that before God, everything we do without Jesus Christ is sin. It is impossible for an unbeliever to do what pleases God because "without faith it is impossible to please God" (Hebrews 11:6). Despite those actions that benefit society, Jesus' words still remain true: "I am the vine; you are the branches. If a man remains in me and I in him, he will bear much fruit; apart from me you can do nothing" (John 15:5). Without a connection to Jesus Christ, we do not have the forgiveness of sins. Then all deeds done even for the good of society are stained by human imperfection and sin. But believers in Jesus cling to the promise of God that the blood of Jesus cleanses us of all sin (1 John 1:7).

Q: **What do we mean when we say that sinful human beings are "unable to reconcile themselves to God"?**

A: Nothing that any human being can do is able to change that person's status before God from sinner to saint, from enemy to friend. We cannot play even the smallest part in making our relationship with God right. Even accepting the reconciling work of Jesus by faith is beyond our powers. "The man without the Spirit [an unbeliever] does not accept the things that come from the Spirit of God, for they are foolishness to him, and he cannot understand them, because they are spiritually discerned" (1 Corinthians 2:14). God determined to reconcile and save us the very same way he created us—with no help from us! Christ suffered for our sins and rose again from the grave. That was God's work and his alone. Then in time God came to us and created faith in our hearts. That was God's work too. "It is because of him that you are in Christ Jesus" (1 Corinthians 1:30).

Q: **If we are born dead in sin and unable to reconcile ourselves to God, how is God just in holding us accountable for our sinfulness?**

A: Every human is born dead to sin, and no one can reconcile himself or herself to God. But God sent Jesus. He reconciled all humanity to himself. All have sinned, but God freely declared all to be righteous because of Christ (Romans 3:23,24). God will hold us accountable for our own sinfulness when we reject God's gift of forgiveness in Christ. When we do not believe in Jesus, in effect we tell God that we don't need his remedy for sin and the victory over death he provided. God's justice has no alternative but to condemn those who reject the solution to sin and death that he freely and graciously provided in Jesus.

6. We believe that God in his gracious providence richly and daily provides for the bodily needs of all people (Psalm 145:15,16). He furthermore protects believers against all danger by keeping evil away from them (Psalm 121:7) or by making it serve their good (Romans 8:28).

Q: If God provides for all people, why do we see so much hunger and starvation in our world?

A: The earth God created produces much more food every year than what is needed to provide for the nutritional needs of the world's population. People in the wealthiest countries of this world waste more in any given year than is needed to feed the hungry. It has happened more than once that political rivals in poor countries leave donated food rotting on loading docks while their own people starve. Sinful human beings' selfishness, greed, and lovelessness towards their fellow human beings play large roles in the hunger many face.

Q: Why does God often allow so many troubles into our lives?

A: We are to think of the cross. We are to think of the fact that "he who did not spare his own Son, but gave him up for us all—how will he not also, along with him, graciously give us all things?" (Romans 8:32). While our troubles, pain, and difficulty may often lead us to cry out as if God's love has failed us, God promises that he will not ever fail us. God's love in Christ gives us only what is good. God spoke to the Old Testament Israelites at one of the most trying times in their history. When they had been taken captive from Judah to Babylon, God promised, "'For I know the plans I have for you,' declares the LORD, 'plans to prosper you and not to harm you, plans to give you hope and a future'" (Jeremiah 29:11). All believers find comfort in these words. In the midst of trouble, we live by faith and not by sight. Even in those troubles God's plans are always to "prosper you and not to harm you."

Q: How can God promise to make evil serve our good when at times the trouble in our lives comes from some sinful decision or action?

A: We can learn from the story of Joseph and his brothers (Genesis 37–47). Neither Joseph nor his brothers were completely innocent. Family rivalries eventually resulted in Joseph's brothers selling Joseph as a slave to merchants on their way to Egypt. And how did God work through all their bitterness and rivalry? When famine broke out, God preserved not just the nation from which he would bring the Savior but also many Egyptians. From all that sin and evil God brought wonderful good.

The same is true in our lives. God's promise that "in all things [he] works for the good of those who love him" (Romans 8:28) is not annulled by our sinfulness. God will bring good from the sinful mistakes we make in our lives. However, that should never be an excuse for us to sin. Even when God allows us to suffer for our mistakes, he has our good in mind. God's forgiving love in Christ is so boundless that he can turn everything—even the results of our sinful stumblings—into blessings for us.

> 7. We reject all theories of evolution as an explanation of the origin of the universe and the human race and all attempts to harmonize the scriptural account of creation with such theories.

Q : Can we harmonize creation and evolution?

A : Creation and evolution express opposite views of the origins of the universe. Creation teaches us that our universe is the wise and majestic plan of our Creator. Evolution teaches that our universe is the result of chance and adaptation. Creation teaches a perfect beginning that was ruined by sin. Evolution teaches a chaotic beginning that has been developing into something better all along. Creation teaches that human beings are special creatures of God, the crown of his creation, possessing unique rational and responsible souls. Evolution teaches that we are only the most highly evolved animals. Creation and evolution represent polar opposites. They are like oil and water. No matter how hard you try to shake them together, they do not mix.

Q : Aren't we closing our eyes to scientific facts when we reject all the theories of evolution?

A: As Christians, we are always open to scientific facts.
We marvel at the advances in medical science and readily welcome new technologies and approaches based on new discoveries in physics, astronomy, biology, and other fields. The Bible encourages such exploration and discovery.

But scientific fact is one thing, and scientific theory is another. It is unfair to suggest that those who believe in God's creation of the universe ignore scientific discovery and close their minds to new research. The presuppositions and assumptions of evolutionary theory provide an explanation of the origins of the universe and humanity without God. Christians believe God provides a better explanation in Genesis and the rest of the Scripture. This too is a presupposition, but it is based on the Scriptures: "The heavens declare the glory of God; the skies proclaim the work of his hands. Day after day they pour forth speech; night after night they display knowledge. There is no speech or language where their voice is not heard. Their voice goes out into all the earth, their words to the ends of the world" (Psalm 19:1-4).

Q: Can I believe in evolution and still believe in the God of the Bible?

A: Every false teaching is a poison that endangers faith.
Living in ignorance of what the Bible says about God's creating activity will never be a benefit to people's faith. In fact, it robs them of the comfort of knowing God's continuing care for them and for the world in which they live. To know what God says and then to choose to believe something different sets a very dangerous course; it suggests that a human can decide which part of the Bible to believe and which part to ignore. God asks us to humbly accept his revelation and to trust him even when we might have some doubts. The Scripture clearly

asserts God's creation and tells us that our Savior is the one "through [whom] all things were made" (John 1:3).

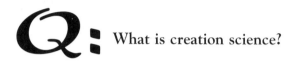 What is creation science?

 Creation science is an attempt to approach the facts and data with the assumption that the world came into existence by God's creative power.

Creation science can be useful when speaking with an unbeliever to demonstrate that belief in creation does not spring from the ravings of irrational minds. At the same time, some of the conclusions and analyses of creation science may be as flawed as those of evolution. In addition, Christians may begin to base their faith on human research instead of God's revelation. The author to the Hebrews proclaims what will always be the reason we confess that we are creatures of a loving and all-powerful Creator: "By faith we understand that the universe was formed at God's command, so that what is seen was not made out of what was visible" (Hebrews 11:3). Since God was the only eyewitness of his creative work, it is "by faith" that we accept his testimony.

8. We reject interpretations that reduce the first chapters of Genesis to a narration of myths or parables or poetic accounts that are not factual history.

Aren't the first chapters of Genesis simply a long parable about our origins and what is the common experience of everyone who has fallen into sin?

$\mathcal{A}$: Nowhere in Genesis 1–3 does the text of Scripture give any hint that we are dealing with anything but the revelation of factual, historical events. And the evidence of the rest of Scripture backs up that conclusion. Genesis 4 and 5 trace the family history of Adam and Eve. In Romans 5, Paul contrasts Adam and Jesus and the effects of their actions on the rest of the whole human race. If Adam is nothing but a mythical man, then Paul's whole point is meaningless. In 2 Corinthians 11:3 Paul speaks of Eve and her fall as a real, historical event that we are in danger of copying.

Claims that the opening portions of the Bible are nothing but myth and parable often come because one is not willing to accept the Genesis record as God's special revelation about the origins of the universe and humanity.

9. We reject all theories that blur the distinction between human beings and animals, since only human beings have immortal souls and are accountable to God.

$\mathcal{Q}$: How do we know that only human beings have immortal souls?

$\mathcal{A}$: First, we would not know anything about this question for sure unless God had told us the truth in his Word. God tells us that only human beings were created in the image of God and are rational, responsible creatures accountable to God. According to the Scripture, only human beings have a spirit that returns to God: "The dust returns to the ground it came from, and the spirit returns to God who gave it" (Ecclesiastes 12:7). Only human beings face judgment: "Man is destined to die once, and after that to face judgment" (Hebrews

9:27). Second, Scripture asserts throughout that humans have unique bodies and souls and have a unique relationship and responsibility to the Creator. Finally, the fact that Jesus' redemption won salvation for all human beings, and only human beings, is further evidence that we are the only two-part—body and soul—creatures that God created.

Q: Can humans abuse other created animals because we are more important than they are?

A: Those who make such claims have an argument with God. He told Adam and Eve, "Be fruitful and increase in number; fill the earth and subdue it. Rule over the fish of the sea and the birds of the air and over every living creature that moves on the ground" (Genesis 1:28). God has indeed given to human beings a position of rule over every other creature.

But we must be quick to point out that our concept of rule is often corrupted. Sinful human beings distort it to mean control for selfish advantage, no matter what harm or pain that may inflict. While using animals for food and clothing is clearly defended by Scripture (Genesis 3:21; Genesis 9:1ff), the careless destruction of God's creatures and the thought-less pollution of the earth's environment are not what God commanded us to do. Our rule of the world is to be patterned after God's perfect ruling.

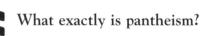

10. We reject all theories that blur the distinction between God and his creation (pantheism).

Q: What exactly is pantheism?

A: Pantheism is the false teaching that "all is God, and God is all." Pantheism denies that there is any difference between the Creator and the creation. It denies the existence of a personal, divine being who is separate from his creation, often substituting some kind of impersonal universal force that pervades everything.

Q: Where would we find those who teach pantheism today?

A: Most eastern religions, such as Hinduism and Buddhism, are pantheistic.

> 11. We reject all views that look upon people as basically good by nature; that consider their natural tendencies to be mere weaknesses, which are not sinful; or that fail to recognize their total spiritual depravity and their inability to please God (Romans 3:9-18).

Q: Don't the concepts of human sin and total spiritual depravity damage self-esteem?

A: If *self-esteem* means "trust in one's own innate goodness and abilities," then God indeed desires not just to damage but to destroy such self-esteem. God says through Jeremiah the prophet, "Cursed is the one who trusts in man, who depends on flesh for his strength and whose heart turns away from the LORD" (17:5). Solomon also asserted, "Trust in the LORD with all your heart and lean not on your own understanding"

(Proverbs 3:5). By trusting in human power and not in God's power and grace we place ourselves under God's curse. This is the proud opposite of humble faith in God.

But of course that is not Scripture's only message. Human self-esteem builds on the love God has for flawed, sinful humans. In the life, death, and resurrection of Jesus Christ, God says of each of us, "You were washed, you were sanctified, you were justified in the name of the Lord Jesus Christ and by the Spirit of our God" (1 Corinthians 6:11). In the water of our baptisms, we received new identities when we were connected to Jesus Christ. Ever since our baptisms, we have enjoyed the status of being holy, righteous, dearly loved children of God.

To build our concept of self in ourselves is a formula for eternal failure. Such self-esteem is a proud fraud and a deception that God's law seeks to burst. But God doesn't knock down our pride in order to see us grovel. He desires that we see ourselves for what we are so that he might lift us up far higher than any self-help program ever could. He desires in his gospel to lift us up forever to the exalted status of his holy children and heirs of eternal life.

Additional Reading for This Section:

God's Providence: He Cares for You by Mark J. Lenz

Man: From Glory to Ashes and Back by Lyle L. Luchterhand

Genesis by John C. Jeske

Creation: God Made All Things by Cleone H. Weigand

Angels and Demons: Have Wings—Will Travel by John D. Schuetze

Section III.

CHRIST AND REDEMPTION

1. We believe that Jesus Christ is the eternal Son of God, one with the Father from all eternity (John 1:1,2). In the course of time, he took a true and complete, yet sinless, human nature to himself (Galatians 4:4) when he was conceived as a holy child in the virgin Mary through a miracle of the Holy Spirit (Luke 1:35). God's angel testified, "What is conceived in her is from the Holy Spirit" (Matthew 1:20). Jesus Christ is unique, for in him the true God and a true human nature are inseparably united in one person, the holy God-man. He is called Immanuel, which means "God with us" (Matthew 1:23).

Q: Why is it so important that Jesus is "one with the Father from all eternity"?

A: Such a statement clearly proclaims the biblical truth that Jesus is fully God, coequal and coeternal with God the Father. Jesus beautifully teaches that truth in Revelation 22:13 when he declares about himself, "I am the Alpha and the Omega, the First and the Last, the Beginning and the End."

The concept is important because of what it assures us about our salvation. Jesus is God and came to earth to rescue us from sin and death. Only God could provide that rescue. The suffering and death of Jesus was payment for all the world's sin because he is "one with the Father from all eternity." No mere human sacrifice would have been enough. The plan of God to save sinful humans is not wishful thinking by humans who are unable to solve the problems of sin and death. It is the plan of God who came to earth to accomplish it. In addition, Jesus came as "one with the Father from all eternity" to teach us what God wanted us to know. Jesus is not just some ethical teacher or example of virtue; he is God, and his words are the words of one who knows God and is God.

Q: **What do we mean by saying that Jesus took a "complete" human nature?**

A: We say that Jesus had a "complete" human nature because he possessed a true human body and soul no different from ours—except that he was without sin. This simple truth is very important. In order for Jesus to be our substitute, he had to be flesh and blood like us. "Since the children have flesh and blood, he too shared in their humanity so that by his death he might destroy him who holds the power of death—that is, the devil. For this reason he had to be made like his brothers in every way, in order that he might become a merciful and faithful high priest in service to God, and that he might make atonement for the sins of the people" (Hebrews 2:14,17).

Q: **How could Jesus have been born a true human being and yet have been sinless?**

A: There is no other explanation than that the same miraculous power of the Holy Spirit that enabled him to be born of a virgin also enabled him to be born without the inherited sinful condition that has been passed down to us from Adam and Eve. Notice how closely the angel Gabriel joins the one miracle with the other as he announces to Mary how she, a virgin, would be able to give birth to a son: "The Holy Spirit will come upon you, and the power of the Most High will over-shadow you. So the holy one to be born will be called the Son of God" (Luke 1:35).

Q: ■ Does Scripture tell us whether Mary had any
      ■ other children after Jesus was born?

A: ▪ We don't know absolutely, but the Scriptures provide a strong indication that Mary did have other children. First, Matthew 1:25 tells us that "[Joseph] had no union with her until she gave birth to a son." The passage suggests that Mary and Joseph carried on a normal married sexual relationship after Jesus was born. The word *until* only assures us of what happened before Jesus was born. Scripture does not give us details of Mary and Joseph's marriage but, rather, focuses on assuring us that the birth of Jesus was an astounding miracle of God.

Second, Jesus' brothers and sisters are mentioned in Scrip-ture (Matthew 12:46 and 13:55; Mark 6:3; and Galatians 1:19). Some believe the Greek word used for "brother" could mean "relative" rather than the normal understanding of the word. While such a use of the word can be found, the mention of those brothers and sisters in close connection with Mary seems to indicate strongly that they were natural-born sons and daughters of Mary and Joseph after the birth of Jesus.

Q: ■ Why was Jesus baptized by John if he was
      ■ sinless?

A: ▪ Jesus certainly didn't receive Baptism in order to have his sins washed away. He was sinless (1 Peter 2:22;

Hebrews 4:15). John the Baptist knew that and hesitated to baptize Jesus. But Jesus had come to earth to be our substitute. Jesus understood what his own words to John revealed: "Let it be so now; it is proper for us to do this to fulfill all righteousness" (Matthew 3:15). The "righteousness" Jesus fulfilled was not some demand of God's law. John's baptism was gospel—the washing away of sins. By being baptized by John, Jesus showed his willingness to stand in the place of sinners. Jesus presented himself as our substitute when he came to John to be baptized at the beginning of his public ministry. He was willing to fulfill the whole work of salvation the Father had given him to do as our Savior.

To put it another way, in the water of the Jordan, the sinless Jesus put himself in the place of sinners like you and me. Because Jesus put himself in our place and forgives us, we stand in his place with his heavenly Father as dearly loved children. Jesus publicly did what he came to do—stand in our place so that we might stand in his. "God made him who had no sin to be sin for us, so that in him we might become the righteousness of God" (2 Corinthians 5:21).

There was also a second purpose served by Jesus' baptism. When the Holy Spirit visibly descended as a dove on Jesus, he marked Jesus as the great Anointed One. (The Greek word *Christ* and the Hebrew word *Messiah* both mean "Anointed One.") The coming of the Holy Spirit gave John the Baptist the certainty that Jesus of Nazareth was indeed the "Lamb of God, who takes away the sin of the world" (John 1:29). John the Baptist was the one who was to prepare the way for the Messiah. He of all men needed such divinely given certainty to complete his task of pointing sinners to Jesus. God had promised John precisely such heavenly proof: "Then John gave this testimony: 'I saw the Spirit come down from heaven as a dove and remain on him. I would not have known him, except that the one who sent me to baptize with water told me, "The man on whom you see the Spirit come down and remain is he who will baptize with the Holy Spirit"'" (John 1:32,33).

2. We believe that Jesus at all times possessed the fullness of the Deity with all divine power, wisdom, and glory (Colossians 2:9). His divinity was evident when he performed miracles (John 2:11). But while he lived on earth, he took on the form of a servant, humbling himself by laying aside the continuous and full display and use of his divine characteristics. During this time he lived as a man among mankind, endured suffering, and humbled himself to the shameful death on the cross (Philippians 2:7,8). We believe that Christ descended into hell to proclaim his victory over Satan (1 Peter 3:18,19). We believe that he rose again from the grave with a glorified body, ascended, and is exalted on high to rule with power over the world, with grace in his church, and with glory in eternity (Philippians 2:9-11).

Q: What does the word *deity* mean?

A: To speak of "the Deity" is to use another name for God or his qualities. To say that Jesus "possessed the fullness of the Deity" is to say that he is truly and fully God.

Q: How did Jesus possess all the divine fullness and yet live here like a normal human being?

A: This question has troubled many since Jesus' earthly life. He often appeared in such great weakness and humility that some wonder if he possessed all the divine "fullness."

During his life here on earth, Jesus chose to humble himself in such a way that his full divine glory and power was not always, or not fully, evident. In Philippians 2:6-8, Paul tells us that although Jesus is fully equal with God the Father, he did not live in such a way to show that off. Instead he took the form "of a servant." He did that willingly so he could suffer and die for the sins of the world. We call this Jesus' *state of humiliation*.

But even during the time he humbled himself, he did not lose or give up equality with God the Father. Jesus always possessed his divine power and glory, he just didn't always, or fully, make use of it as he humbled himself to rescue us. Even during that time, this statement of Colossians 2:9 always remained true about him: "In Christ all the fullness of the Deity lives in bodily form."

During his ministry, Jesus *did* give glimpses of that limitless power and glory he possessed. Every miracle he performed was a brief glimpse of his infinite power. When his face was as bright as the sun during his transfiguration (Matthew 17), he showed the glory that was his as true God.

In all of this, the most important point to remember is his great love for us. How great is his love for us that he would willingly refrain from making use of his power and glory in order to live, suffer, and die so that we might be his brothers and sisters forever!

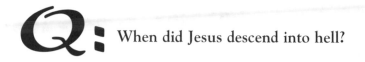 When did Jesus descend into hell?

A: Peter tells us when Jesus' descent took place in 1 Peter 3:18,19: "For Christ died for sins once for all, the righteous for the unrighteous, to bring you to God. He was put to death in the body but made alive by the Spirit, through whom also he went and preached to the spirits in prison." Peter tells us that Jesus went to proclaim his victory in hell after he had been "made alive." While the exact chronology of all the

Easter morning events cannot be stated, Jesus' descent took place sometime early on that first Easter morning.

 Did Jesus descend into hell to give a second chance to the souls who were in hell at that time?

A: Nowhere does 1 Peter 3:18,19 give any indication that the purpose of Jesus' descent was to rescue souls from hell. The word Peter uses for what Jesus did ("preached") means simply "to herald a message." Jesus was doing nothing more in hell than announcing to Satan and the souls there that he, not Satan, had been victorious in the struggle. That he who had been crucified stood there gloriously alive was the greatest proof of the truth of his proclamation.

Also from other Scripture passages we can see that a human being's time of grace ends upon his or her death. Scripture does not hold out the hope of a second chance after death. Jesus' story of the rich man and poor Lazarus (Luke 16:19-31) makes that clear. The rich man had no hope or help after his death. His time of grace was over. The author to the Hebrews also states that quite directly when he writes, "Man is destined to die once, and after that to face judgment" (Hebrews 9:27).

Q: **How can Jesus be with us always if he is in an exalted position in heaven at God's right hand?**

A: When Scripture speaks of God's right hand, it is using a figure of speech. God is a spirit (John 4:24) who has neither left nor right hand. Yet the Scriptures do speak of God's right hand. But God's right hand is not a place. Instead, it is a figure of speech for God's power and authority. It is God's gracious ruling power for the sake of his plan of salvation. Consider Moses' words in Exodus 15:6 just after God had rescued the Israelites from Pharaoh's army at the Red Sea: "Your right hand, O LORD, was majestic in power. Your right hand, O LORD, shattered the enemy." Clearly Moses was not talking about a particular place when he spoke of the Lord's "right hand." But Moses was praising God for his gracious power.

When Scripture says that Jesus is at the "right hand" of God, it is not telling us about his location in the universe. Rather it is assuring us that Jesus, who humbled himself to save us, has resumed using his full power and authority together with the Father and the Holy Spirit. Therefore, since the "right hand" of God is not a place in space but rather a way of speaking of the power of Jesus, he can rule all things while at the same time being with us. What a comforting truth that our Brother who saved us is with us every moment of our lives, wherever we are!

3. We believe that Jesus Christ, the God-man, was sent by the Father to redeem all people, that is, to buy them back from the guilt and punishment of sin. Jesus came to fulfill the law (Matthew 5:17) so that on the basis of his perfect obedience all people would be declared holy (Romans 5:18,19). He came to bear "the iniquity of us all" (Isaiah 53:6), ransoming all people by his sacrifice for sin on the altar of the cross (Matthew 20:28). We believe that he is the God-appointed substitute for all people. His righteousness, or perfect obedience, is accepted by the Father as our righteousness, his death for sin as our death for sin (2 Corinthians 5:21). We believe that his resurrection gives full assurance that God has accepted the payment he made for all (Romans 4:25).

Q: In what way has Jesus fulfilled the law?

A: Our holy and perfect Creator has every right to expect us to be what he created us to be. Human beings were created in his image, holy and perfect. God's law demands perfect love for both God and our neighbors. That is precisely how Jesus summed up what God's law justly asks of us: "One of them, an expert in the law, tested him with this question: 'Teacher, which is the greatest commandment in the Law?' Jesus replied: '"Love the Lord your God with all your heart and with all your soul and with all your mind." This is the first and greatest commandment. And the second is like it: "Love your neighbor as yourself"'" (Matthew 22:35-39).

Sadly, all of that is completely out of reach for every one of us. We were born with a sinful nature that was dead in sin and hostile to God, and we have daily proven countless times that we are far from perfect.

But Jesus has fulfilled God's law as our substitute. He willingly placed himself under the same law we break. Throughout his 33 years of earthly life, he never once failed to offer perfect love to his heavenly Father and perfect love to everyone else as well. Jesus could boldly say even to his enemies, "Can any of you prove me guilty of sin?" (John 8:46).

The righteous life of Jesus perfectly fulfilled every demand of God's law. In addition, Jesus took our place and paid the penalty we deserve for our failure to do as God requires. He is our full and complete substitute. In other words, just as his death paid for our sins against God's law, so also his life gave us his record of keeping the demands of the law. When we believe in what Jesus did, we receive the benefits of his work. As God looks at us, he sees his Son's perfect obedience and counts us as those who have met every demand of his law. Perhaps nowhere is that more simply summed up than in 2 Corinthians 5:21: "God made him who had no sin to be sin for us, so that in him we might become the righteousness of God."

Q: In what way does Jesus' resurrection from the dead give us "full assurance that God has accepted the payment he made for all"?

A: God the Father had entrusted the work of being the world's Savior to his Son. The Son of God took on our human flesh and blood and lived and died to complete that work of salvation. In his own words on Calvary, the Son of God declared, "It is finished" (John 19:30).

Easter morning was God the Father's stamp of approval on his Son's work. Death could not hold Jesus. Instead he arose from the dead. Paul wrote, "He was delivered over to death for our sins and was raised to life for our justification" (Romans 4:25). The apostle asserts that Jesus died because our sins were upon him. But when Jesus arose on Easter morning, God was declaring that what he had done was enough to declare sinners not guilty. The empty tomb of Easter morning was proof positive that "there is now no condemnation for those who are in Christ Jesus" (Romans 8:1).

Q: Does the Bible claim that Jesus died even for people who will never believe in him?

A: One of the most familiar passages of all of Scripture (John 3:16) reminds us that God gave his one and only Son for "the world" so that "whoever believes in him shall not perish but have eternal life." Faith in Jesus does not make him the Savior; Jesus is already the Savior of the world. Faith is the individual, personal claim on what Jesus has already done. That's why what Jesus has done can be sure and certain for "whoever believes in him."

God leaves no doubt about that truth. The Bible says, "God was reconciling the world to himself in Christ, not counting men's sins against them. And he has committed to us the message of reconciliation" (2 Corinthians 5:19). All sins of all people—the world—were counted against Christ. The only thing that needs to be done is to announce this completed reconciliation between God and the world. Whether people believe the message or not, it is true. Faith claims the reconciliation. Unbelief fails to claim it and loses its blessings.

Peter wrote, "But there were also false prophets among the people, just as there will be false teachers among you. They will secretly introduce destructive heresies, even denying the sovereign Lord who bought them—bringing swift destruction on themselves" (2 Peter 2:1). Notice that these false prophets will end up in eternal destruction, but that does not change the fact that the Lord himself "bought them."

4. We believe that God reconciled "the world to himself in Christ, not counting men's sins against them" (2 Corinthians 5:19). We believe that Jesus is "the Lamb of God, who takes away the sin of the world" (John 1:29). The mercy and grace of God are all-embracing; the reconciliation through Christ is universal; the forgiveness of sins has been gained as an accomplished fact for all people. Because of the substitutionary work of Christ, God has justified all people, that is, God has declared them to be not guilty. This forms the firm, objective basis for the sinner's assurance of salvation.

Q: Why do we repeatedly ask God to forgive our sins if our forgiveness of sins has already been gained by Christ?

A: Daily confession is not something we do for God's benefit—as if we have to somehow plead with him to be willing to forgive us. Confession of sins is important because we still live with a sinful nature. Because of that sinful nature, we have a tendency to grow comfortable with sin and neglect the forgiveness Jesus won for us. Therefore, when we confess our sins each day, we turn from the sins that want to choke our faith in Christ's grace and renew our faith in the forgiveness of sins secured long ago by Christ. That regular activity strengthens our faith so that we might live as God expects. It is what Paul urges us to do in Galatians 5:24: "Those who belong to Christ Jesus have crucified the sinful nature with its passions and desires."

Q: Why is it so important to have an "objective basis" for our assurance of salvation?

A: If some part of salvation, even the smallest part, depended on us, we could never be certain that we had done our part well enough to be right with God. But the Scriptures describe the work of salvation as a completed fact—an objective reality that does not depend on any human action, thought, or desire. It is certain because it depends completely on the life, death, and resurrection of the Son of God and not on us. Because our salvation is all done and was accomplished by God himself, we find certainty and security in our doubts and in life's highs and lows.

5. We reject any teaching that in any way limits Christ's work of atonement. We reject any teaching that says Christ paid the penalty only for the sins of some people. We reject any teaching that says Christ made only a partial payment for sins.

Q: Why do some try to limit Christ's work of atonement?

A: Since not all people will be saved, people have forever tried to come up with human theories about why some are saved and some are not. Some incorrectly conclude that if God really wanted all people to be saved, then all would be going to heaven. They continue with the thought that since all will not be going to heaven, God must not really want all people to be saved. If that is true, they claim, then Jesus only died for those who will be found in heaven forever. Those who will be lost are lost because God never really wanted them and because Jesus didn't die for them. But God has redeemed the world, and those who reject God's full and complete redemption are lost by their own fault because they failed to believe it.

6. We reject the views that consider the Gospel accounts to be pious fiction developed by early Christians to express their ideas about Jesus Christ rather than a true account of what actually happened in history. We reject all attempts to make the historical accuracy of events in Christ's life—such as his virgin birth, his miracles, or his bodily resurrection—appear unimportant or even doubtful. We reject the attempts to stress a "present encounter with the living Christ" in such a way that Jesus' redemptive work recorded in Scripture loses its importance.

 Q: How do we know that the Scriptures are more than pious fiction developed by the early church?

A: The best answer for that question was given long ago by Peter in his second letter: "We did not follow cleverly invented stories when we told you about the power and coming of our Lord Jesus Christ, but we were eyewitnesses of his majesty. For he received honor and glory from God the Father when the voice came to him from the Majestic Glory, saying, 'This is my Son, whom I love; with him I am well pleased.' We ourselves heard this voice that came from heaven when we were with him on the sacred mountain. And we have the word of the prophets made more certain, and you will do well to pay attention to it, as to a light shining in a dark place, until the day dawns and the morning star rises in your hearts. Above all, you must understand that no prophecy of Scripture came about by the prophet's own interpretation. For prophecy never had its origin in the will of man, but men spoke from God as they were carried along by the Holy Spirit" (1:16-21).

It is more than just passing interest to note as well that those who testified to these truths were willing to die for the truth of what they taught. That should not surprise us, because as Peter points out, they were not sharers of pious fiction but eyewitnesses to the glory of our Savior.

Q: **What does a "present encounter with the living Christ" mean, and what is the danger of such an emphasis?**

A: Those who speak of a "present encounter with the living Christ" point to the experience one might have with Christ. This approach points away from the reliability of the objective, written truth of the gospel message. Instead, Jesus does not become real and personal until some kind of subjective experience validates that he is our Savior. Such teaching places us on the sandy ground of the human heart instead of on the unmovable solid rock of God's objective truth. Our experiences

and opinions about the message of Christ become more important than the inspired witness of the gospel itself.

Additional Reading for This Section:

Matthew by G. J. Albrecht and M. J. Albrecht
Mark by Harold E. Wicke
Luke by Victor H. Prange
John by Gary P. Baumler
The Life of Christ by Armin J. Panning
We Believe in Jesus Christ: Essays on Christology edited by Curtis A. Jahn

Section IV.
JUSTIFICATION BY GRACE THROUGH FAITH

1. We believe that God has justified all sinners, that is, he has declared them righteous for the sake of Christ. This is the central message of Scripture upon which the very existence of the church depends. It is a message relevant to people of all times and places, of all races and social levels, for "the result of one trespass was condemnation for all men" (Romans 5:18). All need forgiveness of sins before God, and Scripture proclaims that all have been justified, for "the result of one act of righteousness was justification that brings life for all men" (Romans 5:18).

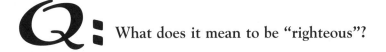 What does it mean to be "righteous"?

When God created Adam and Eve, he created them "in his own image" (Genesis 1:27). They were both righteous, that is, in perfect harmony with God. To be "righteous" means to be "sinless and perfect." Anyone who is righteous can stand before God without fear of his judgment. The psalm writer describes that state of righteousness this way: "Who may ascend the hill of the LORD? Who may stand in his holy place? He who has clean hands and a pure heart" (Psalm 24:3,4).

Q : What does it mean to be declared righteous?

A : None of us could ever attain the status of being perfect and holy (righteous) in God's sight. ("There is no one righteous, not even one; there is no one who understands, no one who seeks God" [Romans 3:10,11].) Yet God provided a way in which we can still receive the status of being considered righteous before him. "God made [Jesus] who had no sin to be sin for us, so that in him we might become the righteousness of God" (2 Corinthians 5:21). God the Father "made him . . . to be sin for us" by considering Jesus to be guilty in our place, for every sin of every person of all time. God considered the suffering and death of Jesus as the punishment for all the sins of the world. But that is not all. God also credited the perfect life of Jesus to sinners. In this way we "become the righteousness of God."

Because of his love for all humanity, Jesus stepped forward to accept the guilt of our sins against God and offered his perfect life as the righteous life God required. Picture a courtroom. We stand guilty, but Jesus steps forward and willingly takes the penalty for us. We go free, and God considers us righteous. That is the declaration that has occurred in God's courtroom. God now views us as righteous by this exchange of sin and holiness between Jesus and each one of us.

Q : Why do we say that justification is the "central message of Scripture"?

A : God planned the justification of humanity from the first sin in the Garden of Eden, and the story of the Bible is how God carried out his plan. Not only is justification central to all of Scripture, it is also central to every sinner.

Without what Jesus has done to justify us, we cannot stand in a right relationship with God. All sinners would be condemned without God's declaration of acquittal, or justification. In addition, through the message of our justification (being declared righteous), the Holy Spirit works faith in our hearts. Only through faith in Jesus' justifying life, death, and resurrection do we receive acquittal from sin as our personal possession.

Q: How can we say that all have been justified when billions don't believe in Jesus?

A: Justification, or the declaration of acquittal, is God's gift to all humanity. He has provided it freely and without any consideration of any human effort. It is like any gift offered in love. But like any gift, it doesn't do any good unless you possess it as yours. Faith makes God's gift yours. When billions do not believe in Jesus, they simply refuse God's gift. All have been justified by God's free grace, but not all make it theirs by faith.

Scripture tells us about the importance of sharing the message of forgiveness in Christ. Paul wrote, "God was reconciling the world to himself in Christ, not counting men's sins against them. And he has committed to us the message of reconciliation. We are therefore Christ's ambassadors, as though God were making his appeal through us. We implore you on Christ's behalf: Be reconciled to God" (2 Corinthians 5:19,20). Clearly Paul says that the whole world has been reconciled to God, but not everyone believes. The billions without Jesus need to hear of God's acquittal of sinners in Christ. Sharing that message brings faith in the hearts of some. Therefore, Paul writes about being ambassadors who share God's message. Through those who are already believers, God continues to urge others to believe and "be reconciled to

God." Whether a sinner believes in Jesus or not does not change the fact of what God has done at the cross of his Son. The only thing that changes is whether a sinner continues to live in hostility toward God or through faith enjoys living in a reconciled relationship with God. Unbelief refuses to enjoy what Christ has done. Unbelief takes the priceless gift of for-giveness and righteousness that God has given to all sinners and throws it away!

2. We believe that individuals receive this free gift of forgiveness not on the basis of their own works, but only through faith (Ephesians 2:8,9). Justifying faith is trust in Christ and his redemptive work. This faith justifies not because of any power it has in itself, but only because of the salvation prepared by God in Christ, which it embraces (Romans 3:28; 4:5). On the other hand, although Jesus died for all, Scripture says that "whoever does not believe will be condemned" (Mark 16:16). Unbelievers forfeit the forgiveness won for them by Christ (John 8:24).

Q: Isn't my faith the small contribution I make to my own salvation?

A: That would be a valid and rational conclusion to make if Scripture pictured faith as a work that we do. Instead, everywhere in Scripture faith is described as a gift of the Holy Spirit. We can do nothing to deserve God's decla-ration. Even faith does not contribute to our salvation. It only receives what God has accomplished and given. The apostle Paul wrote, "For it is by grace you have been saved, through faith—and this not from yourselves, it is the gift of God—not by works, so that no one can boast" (Ephesians 2:8,9). The Scriptures maintain that faith and works are opposites. To say that we are saved through faith is to say that we are saved without one work—even one small work. Paul emphasized this point also in Romans 4:4,5: "Now when a man works, his wages are not credited to him as a gift, but as an obligation. However, to the man who does not work but trusts God who justifies the wicked, his faith is credited as righteousness." Scripture is consistent in presenting faith as God's gift that saves us without even the least contribution on our part.

The question comes from our human struggle with the pride of our sinful nature. We want to take at least some credit for our salvation instead of bowing to the humbling conclusion that we could do nothing. To our sinful nature, this will always remain a part of what Paul calls "the offense of the cross" (Galatians 5:11).

Q: **What does it mean that faith doesn't have any "power . . . in itself"?**

A: Faith has no power in itself. In other words, faith is not such a noble or good human effort that it moves God to love the one who has faith. Instead, faith simply trusts what God has already done. The "power" of faith is in that which it trusts (its object) and not in itself.

For instance, children have faith that their mothers and fathers will provide food, clothing, and shelter. The children live every day with this absolute faith. When they arrive at home for dinner, the meal is on the table ready to eat. Their faith has not provided the meal. Instead, the parents have provided it by buying the food and preparing it. It is not the faith but the object of that faith. Of course, the faith of a child is valuable and important, but it has no power to put food on the table. The power of faith is in that to which it clings—not in the faith itself. We don't have faith in faith. We have faith in Jesus Christ.

Of course, sometimes our faith is weak and we are filled with doubts. God assures us of his love and forgiveness, but sometimes we wonder if it's true. It is very important to understand that the blessings God has promised do not depend on how strong our faith is. In fact, because of our stubborn sinful nature with its doubts, the hardest thing for a believer to believe is that he or she believes! That is why it is so comforting to be directed not to our faith but to our Savior. As our eyes are lifted to his cross and the depth of his saving love—the object of our faith—our faith is strengthened. We so frequently must join our voices to say the simple prayer of a man who once came to Jesus: "I do believe; help me overcome my unbelief!" (Mark 9:24).

Q: Since all have been justified, why don't all go to heaven whether they believe or not?

A: John 3:16 is very familiar to many people. If we listen to that passage with its following verses, we have Jesus' own answer to our question: "God so loved the world that he gave his one and only Son, that whoever believes in him shall not perish but have eternal life. For God did not send his Son into the world to condemn the world, but to save the world through him. Whoever believes in him is not condemned, but whoever does not believe stands condemned already because he has not believed in the name of God's one and only Son." To refuse to believe in Jesus Christ is to call God a liar. Such rejection of the very message that saves will condemn people forever.

3. We believe that people cannot produce this justify-ing faith, or trust, in their own hearts, because "the man without the Spirit does not accept the things that come from the Spirit of God, for they are foolishness to him" (1 Corinthians 2:14). In fact, "the sinful mind is hostile to God" (Romans 8:7). It is the Holy Spirit who gives people faith to recognize that "Jesus is Lord" (1 Corinthi-ans 12:3). The Holy Spirit works this faith by means of the gospel (Romans 10:17). We believe, therefore, that a person's conversion is entirely the work of God's grace. Rejection of the gospel is, however, entirely the unbe-liever's own fault (Matthew 23:37).

Q ■ Why is the gospel foolishness to an unbe-
    ■ liever?

A ■ The good news of Christ is foolishness to an unbe-liever chiefly because of "the offense of the cross" (Galatians 5:11). The Scriptures proclaim that every human is conceived and born as a sinner who is hostile to God. The Scriptures also proclaim that the only way for any human to be saved is through the suffering and death of Jesus. Natural human pride ridicules such teachings as foolishness because it desires to claim some human contribution toward its status before God. Consider how every other "religion" other than true Christian-ity is based on the teaching that in some way we can make our-selves acceptable—at times with great effort and expense—to whoever god is. Unbelievers reject the gospel as foolishness because it calls all reliance on human goodness useless. Christ has done everything necessary for salvation.

There are also other reasons human sinful nature rejects the gospel as foolishness. Every miracle of the gospel appears to be foolishness. Human logic and thought consider God's miracles foolish, such as the Son of God taking on a real human nature, Jesus' resurrection from the dead, and the inspiration of Scripture by the Holy Spirit. The miracles of the Holy Spirit using plain water in Baptism or bread and wine in the Lord's Supper to work wonderful blessings of grace do not make sense to unbelievers. How thankful we are that "the foolishness of God is wiser than man's wisdom, and the weakness of God is stronger than man's strength" (1 Corinthians 1:25).

Q: **If I can reject Jesus, don't I also have the power to accept him?**

A: While we cannot deny that such an argument seems reasonable to human logic, that argument fails in one particularly important point: It is not what the Bible says. Every one of us entered this life dead in sin (Ephesians 2:1), hostile to God (Romans 8:7), and thinking the gospel is nothing but foolishness (1 Corinthians 2:14). We had absolutely no spiritual power to move toward God. We could only run from him and hide—even while God was tracking us down and calling to us with the very message that saves us. God then performed the miracle of faith within us. "God, who is rich in mercy, made us alive with Christ even when we were dead in transgressions" (Ephesians 2:4,5; see also Colossians 2:13).

In 1 Corinthians 1:26-31 Paul repeatedly emphasizes that God chose us and that we did not choose him. Paul's whole point is that we don't have reason to be proud because we did not choose God or accept him. But we have reason for praise and thanks because God did it all for us, including giving us the gift of faith in his Son. That's why Paul concludes that section by saying, "Therefore, as it is written: 'Let him who boasts boast in the Lord'" (1 Corinthians 1:31).

Q: How does the Holy Spirit use the gospel to bring people to faith?

A: "Faith comes from hearing the message, and the message is heard through the word of Christ" (Romans 10:17). Every time the message of the gospel is read, heard, and remembered, the Holy Spirit is at work. Every time the gospel is heard, seen, touched, and tasted in the sacraments (Baptism and Lord's Supper), the Holy Spirit is at work. The Holy Spirit uses these sacraments to create or strengthen faith in Jesus Christ. The Bible confirms this point: "But we ought always to thank God for you, brothers loved by the Lord, because from the beginning God chose you to be saved through the sanctifying work of the Spirit and through belief in the truth. He called you to this through our gospel, that you might share in the glory of our Lord Jesus Christ" (2 Thessalonians 2:13,14). Notice how the Holy Spirit is pictured as working through the gospel's message. God tells us that the gospel is his power: "I am not ashamed of the gospel, because it is the power of God for the salvation of everyone who believes" (Romans 1:16).

We call the gospel in Word and sacrament the means of grace because the Holy Spirit uses these tools, or means, to create and strengthen faith in God's grace. God has not promised that he will work in any other way than through these means of grace. Therefore, it is important for believers to use the gospel by attending worship services and having regular personal or family devotions.

Q: If God wants all people to be saved and saving faith is a gift of the Holy Spirit, why hasn't God simply given this gift to all people?

A: Often this question is asked because of doubts about God's desire to save all people and about faith as a gift of the

Holy Spirit. Since God has clearly not given saving faith to all people, some insist that logic indicates that this must be because God does not really want all people to be saved. The other option is that humans must have some cooperative role in coming to faith. This option could be restated this way: some are saved because they cooperate at least a little bit with the Spirit in their conversion; others are lost because they do not cooperate with the Spirit.

But this is one of those many places where human reason must give way to God's superior revelation. God's Word clearly states both that God wants all people to be saved (for example, Isaiah 45:22; Ezekiel 33:11; John 3:16; 2 Corinthians 5:14-21; 1 Timothy 2:3,4) and that faith is the gift of the Holy Spirit (see answer to previous question).

The fact that some people do not possess saving faith is not because God does not want those people. Jesus places the responsibility for unbelief squarely and only on those who continue to reject the offered gospel (Matthew 23:37-39). At the same time, a believer trusts God's promises because of the power of the Holy Spirit working through the means of grace. Believers do not resist less than unbelievers nor do they cooperate more. Claiming that if we can resist the gospel, we must also have the power to accept it is humanly logical but biblically indefensible. Nowhere does Scripture speak of lesser resistance on the part of some and greater resistance on the part of others. By nature all are equally dead in sin, hostile to God, and consider the gospel to be foolishness.

If someone is saved through faith in Jesus, God deserves all the credit. If someone is lost because of unbelief, the sinner is totally responsible. Beyond that, Scripture does not allow us to speculate. If we go beyond what God tells us in the Scriptures, we forget that God's ways and logic are far beyond us. "'For my thoughts are not your thoughts, neither are your ways my ways,' declares the LORD. 'As the heavens are higher than the earth, so are my ways higher than your ways and my thoughts than your thoughts'" (Isaiah 55:8,9).

4. We believe that sinners are saved by grace alone. Grace is the undeserved love of God for sinners. This love led God to give sinners everything they need for their salvation. It is all a gift of God. People do nothing to earn any of it (Ephesians 2:8,9).

Q : Why are we so careful to say that we don't take any credit for any part of our salvation?

A : When we begin to think that we play even a small part for our own salvation, we set ourselves up for either pride or despair.

First, someone might take pride in contributing to salvation. But taking pride in something we have done is the opposite of faith in Christ. Pride over what we do in our relationship with God asserts that we desire to find our salvation in law, that is, in what we do, rather than in gospel, that is, in what Christ has done. In Galatians, Paul warns us of the awful results of such spiritual pride: "You who are trying to be justified by law have been alienated from Christ; you have fallen away from grace" (5:4).

But thinking that our salvation depends on us in any way also can lead to the exact opposite problem: despair. As soon as anyone begins to believe that salvation depends on any human effort or inclination, doubts arise. One may wonder if he or she has done enough to please God. Even an emphasis on making a "decision for Christ" can bring uncertainty. One might wonder if the decision was really valid or if it was only made at a time of emotional excitement.

The only safe path is the one Scripture holds before us: Everything for our salvation has been accomplished by Christ, even our faith is itself a gift of the Holy Spirit. Believers find great comfort in God's gifts of salvation and faith. Believers base their comfort not on their emotions, decisions, or efforts but on the objective certainty of God's love at the cross and empty tomb of Jesus.

> 5. We believe that already before the world was created, God chose those individuals whom he would in time convert through the gospel of Christ and preserve in faith to eternal life (Ephesians 1:4-6; Romans 8:29,30). This election to faith and salvation in no way was caused by anything in people but shows how completely salvation is by grace alone (Romans 11:5,6).

Q: **How can the Bible say that God wants all people to be saved and that he elected some to be saved from eternity?**

A: Both statements are clearly biblical. God's Word clearly proclaims that he equally desires all people to be saved and sent his Son to bleed and die for every last sinner (Isaiah 45:22; Ezekiel 33:11; John 3:16; 2 Corinthians 5:14-21; 1 Timothy 2:3,4). God's Word also clearly proclaims that from all eternity, God—by pure grace alone—elected some to be brought to faith in Jesus, preserved in faith, and brought home to heaven (Romans 8:29,30; Ephesians 1:3-14).

While those two truths seem to contradict each other, once again we must remember that God has never promised that his reason and logic will make sense to us. Since we live by faith and not by sight, God asks us to trust that he is still faithful and just even when we cannot understand all that he does.

When believers are confronted by these difficulties, they recall words such as these from Psalm 131: "My heart is not proud, O LORD, my eyes are not haughty; I do not concern myself with great matters or things too wonderful for me. But I have stilled and quieted my soul; like a weaned child with its mother, like a weaned child is my soul within me. O Israel, put your hope in the LORD both now and forevermore" (verses 1-3). Our Father in heaven reveals many things that are beyond our full grasp. Yet notice how the psalm ends— not in frustration but in hope.

Q: **Why is our election not "caused by anything in people"?**

A: The doctrine of election is one of the most powerful proofs that we are saved completely by grace and not by anything in us. Paul clearly talks about election in Ephesians 1:4: "For he chose us in him before the creation of the world to be holy and blameless in his sight." Notice that God elected us before the creation of the universe. From his vantage point of eternity, God looked ahead, saw us, and chose us. What he saw from eternity was the fall into sin of all humankind. He saw that we would be born as sinful rebels. But despite the sin he saw, he chose us. He didn't choose us because we were different, as if somehow we were already holy and blameless. But as Paul tells us, out of pure grace alone God chose us "*to be* holy and blameless in his sight."

Q: **How can I be sure that I am one of God's elect?**

A: God does not permit us to peer into eternity to see him at work, choosing us to be his own. We cannot look into heaven either to see ourselves there for eternity. But the Scriptures explain God's actions in this way: "For those God foreknew he also predestined to be conformed to the likeness of his Son, that he might be the firstborn among many brothers. And those he predestined, he also called; those he called, he also justified; those he justified, he also glorified" (Romans 8:29,30). In this passage God promises to work in the lives of his people, his elect. In their baptisms, he has "called" them to faith as his children. By his Holy Spirit, he has taught them to trust that they are his "justified" sons and daughters who have Jesus as their brother. What God has done in the lifetimes of his elect is evidence that he will also glorify them in the resurrection from the dead. He will gather his own and give them places in his glorious mansions in heaven. Picture Romans 8:29,30 as a "golden chain" of God's activity for believers from eternity, in time, and to all eternity. This golden chain links what God has done in the lives of believers now to what he did in eternity and will still do for them for eternity. The passage gives believers the powerful comfort of God's gracious activity on their behalf already before they were born, stretching onward to their eternal lives in heaven. You are one of God's elect because God has promised you forgiveness and life in Jesus and made you a believer.

Q: **If God is going to get all of his elect home to heaven one way or another, why is it so important that we share our faith with those who don't know Jesus?**

A: Included in God's election was also the message, means, and method through and by which he would call, gather, and preserve his elect children. Notice in Ephesians 1:9 what was included in his electing love: "And he made known to us the mystery of his will according to his good pleasure, which he purposed in Christ." He brings his elect to faith as he makes known to them "his good pleasure, which he purposed in Christ." That "good pleasure" is the message of Jesus Christ, the means of grace or the gospel in Word and sacrament. And how does the message reach God's elect? God simply uses those who are already his children to share the message of the gospel. In that way God wondrously gives believers a part to play in the fulfillment of his electing love!

6. We believe that at the moment of death, the souls of those who believe in Christ go immediately to be with the Lord in the joy of heaven because of the atoning work of Christ (Luke 23:43). The souls of those who do not believe in Christ go to an eternity of misery in hell (Luke 16:22-24).

Q: Some teach that after we die, our souls sleep with our bodies until judgment day. Why don't we teach such "soul sleep"?

A: When Jesus tells the story of the rich man and poor Lazarus (Luke 16:19-31), neither Lazarus nor the rich man were asleep in the grave. Instead, Lazarus was in heaven aware of his great blessings and the rich man was in hell fully aware of his suffering. At the same time, the rich man's brothers continued to live on earth. When Jesus spoke to the thief on the cross, he said, "I tell you the truth, today you will be with me in paradise" (Luke 23:43). The thief's body long ago returned to dust and is now waiting for judgment day, yet his soul has been with Jesus in heaven since the first Good Friday. In addition, Revelation 6:9ff shows us the souls of the martyrs waiting for judgment day. We are aware that they are in heaven and that God's final judgment has not yet come.

Q: **If souls go immediately to heaven or hell at the moment of death, what is the purpose of judgment day?**

A: Judgment day is not for God's benefit, as if on that day God will decide for the first time what he's going to do with all people for eternity. For all those who already died, that part of judgment will have already been determined. Judgment day will make God's judgment public and evident to all humanity of all time. All will understand that God's judgments are just and merciful. In addition, Jesus will publicly commend his believers for the works they did in his name while denouncing the unbelievers for their failure to live for him.

For those souls who are already in heaven and hell before judgment day, the only thing that will change is that they will continue there forever as soul *and* body.

Q: **What will it be like to be a soul without a body if we die before judgment day?**

A: Scripture gives us no details about the conditions of the soul between death and judgment day. But enjoying the presence of Jesus—even as a soul without a body—will be far more glorious than anything we can imagine. In Philippians, Paul assures us that such an existence with Christ is a great gain compared to life in a sin-troubled world. As Paul discussed his impending trial before Caesar and the possibility of his execution, he wrote, "For to me, to live is Christ and to die is gain. If I am to go on living in the body, this will mean fruitful labor for me. Yet what shall I choose? I do not know! I am torn between the two: I desire to depart and be with Christ, which is better by far; but it is more necessary for you that I remain in the body" (Philippians 1:21-24).

7. We reject every teaching that people in any way contribute to their salvation. We reject the belief that people with their own power can cooperate in their conversion or make a decision for Christ (John 15:16). We reject the belief that those who are converted were less resistant to God's grace than those who remain unconverted. We reject all efforts to present faith as a condition people must fulfill to complete their justification. We reject all attempts of sinners to justify themselves before God.

Q: If someone believes that he or she contributes to salvation in a very small way, has that person lost saving faith in Jesus?

A: Because we have a sinful nature, we daily wrestle with the idea that we contribute something to our salvation. But struggling against such thoughts and agreeing with them are two vastly different things.

The Galatian Christians struggled against false teachers after Paul left them. Those false teachers were called Judaizers, and they taught that faith in Christ's life, death, and resurrection was not enough. Faith in Jesus was a good start. It did almost everything, but you also needed to be circumcised and continue to follow at least some of the Old Testament ceremonial laws of the Jews in order to become a full child of God. Paul wrote some strong words to those who believed the Judaizers' message of Jesus' gospel plus a little human effort: "You who are trying to be justified by law have been alienated from Christ; you have fallen away from grace" (Galatians 5:4). Indeed, to believe that we can contribute to our salvation is to throw away the grace of Jesus Christ. We are either saved by grace alone or by works. There is no middle ground—no both/and.

Q: Why do we reject the teaching that we can cooperate in our conversion or make a decision for Christ?

A: We are so careful to reject any cooperation in conversion because of the spiritual peril that occurs when someone believes that false teaching. That false teaching makes someone vulnerable to the twin spiritual dangers of pride and despair.

The greatest reason for rejecting these ideas is that both of them seek to retain some human credit for the spiritual gifts God provides. First, we believe that Jesus Christ has secured our forgiveness and victory over death by grace. We could not earn those gifts by our efforts. Instead they are free gifts of God to humanity (Romans 3:21-24). A decision for Christ seeks to add some small human effort to an individual's salvation. That position implies that Christ's work is not complete or finished until one makes the decision to believe. It makes salvation depend on the decision rather than on the grace of God in Christ. Second, because we are spiritually dead by birth (Ephesians 2:1-10), we cannot choose Christ or come to God. Faith is God's gift to us too; the Holy Spirit reveals the truth to the natural human mind (1 Corinthians 2:6-16) through the gospel, which is the power of God creating faith within each human heart (Romans 1:16). When one claims to cooperate in conversion or to make a decision for Christ, that person asserts that human beings are not dead in sin. Instead they have some life, even if it is only a little.

The dual dangers of pride and despair often follow. Pride enters the human heart when one claims to take credit for his or her own salvation—deciding and choosing puts human effort into conversion where only God's grace belongs. Despair sometimes follows—teaching some kind of cooperation in conversion foolishly and dangerously inserts a part *you* must fulfill in God's plan for *your* salvation. One wonders if he or she has done enough, and despair and confusion arise in moments of doubt and temptation. When we add a human element to our salvation and make it anything less than a full and complete gift of God, we take our eyes off the certainty of the cross and focus our attention on the uncertainties of human actions and decisions.

Q: **Why do we reject the teaching that some resist the Holy Spirit less than others, since that seems to make sense in understanding why some come to faith and others do not?**

A: We were all dead in sin (Ephesians 2:1) and hostile to God (Romans 8:7). God tells us clearly, "What shall we conclude then? Are we any better? Not at all! We have already made the charge that Jews and Gentiles alike are all under sin. As it is written: 'There is no one righteous, not even one; there is no one who understands, no one who seeks God. All have turned away, they have together become worthless'" (Romans 3:9-12). This unbiblical idea that believers must resist less than those who continue in unbelief is just a more refined version of cooperation in conversion, which is addressed in the previous question. The same problems of pride and despair apply here as well. If believers resist less, then they must be better than unbelievers somehow. But believers are not better or less hostile to God. Instead it is a miracle of God's grace that any humans, who are equally "all under sin," believe.

Q: **Why do we refuse to label saving faith a "condition people must fulfill"?**

A: Such terminology makes faith sound like "one little work" we do to complete God's plan of salvation. God's work of salvation has been complete since Good Friday (John 19:30). Jesus is already the Savior of the world (John 3:16). All sins have been paid for, and Christ's righteousness has been declared to be the property of the world (2 Corinthians 5:14ff). Our faith is not some "condition" we must fulfill in order to make our forgiveness and salvation valid. Faith is nothing more than the Spirit-worked confidence that holds on to the gift of salvation that is already sure, certain, and complete. Faith is not a condition to fulfill but rather a confidence in what Christ has already fulfilled.

Q: **Why is every attempt of sinners to justify themselves before God always a complete failure?**

A: Here's why: Every attempt of sinners to justify themselves is the arrogant pride of a spiritually dead sinner telling God that his Son died for nothing. "If righteousness could be gained through the law, Christ died for nothing!" (Galatians 2:21).

8. We reject any suggestion that the doctrine of justification by faith is no longer meaningful today.

Q: **Why would someone claim that the doctrine of justification "is no longer meaningful today"?**

A: Ultimately, here's why someone would claim that: "For the time will come when men will not put up with sound doctrine. Instead, to suit their own desires, they will gather around them a great number of teachers to say what their itching ears want to hear" (2 Timothy 4:3). The doctrine of justification is greatly offensive to human pride. As sinful human beings ignore their own consciences, which warn that things are not right with God, and attempt to lose themselves only in the issues and concerns of life in this world, they lose any focus on forgiveness before God, resurrection from the dead, and eternal life. Will anyone who stands before Jesus on the Last Day say that justification "is no longer meaningful today"?

9. We reject the teaching that believers can never fall from faith ("once saved, always saved"), because the Bible says it is possible for believers to fall from faith (1 Corinthians 10:12).

Q: God has elected from eternity some who will be preserved in faith to eternal life, and yet it is possible for a believer to fall from faith. How can this be?

A: A believer of a past generation succinctly and beautifully answered this difficult question:

Reason finds it impossible to see how the man who is convinced that he can fall, that he may fall, that he is in great danger of falling away throughout his earthly life, can also be perfectly sure that he will never fall away.

One answer that Lutheranism gives is that the contradictory heart of man needs a contradictory doctrine. . . . Thus the Christian must learn to live in constant tension between these two. When he begins to lean over to the left, toward pride and presumption and confidence in the strength of his faith, and to trust in his own character, then the warnings against apostasy, the Savior's, "Watch and pray, lest ye enter into temptation" pushes him upright once more. But usually man, even the Christian man, whose heart is never fully what it ought to be, begins then to lean over to the right—he becomes afraid and begins to doubt that he will ever make it to the gates of the heavenly city. Once again the Savior comes and stands on the other side to support him and to push him upright once more with his promise, "Do not fear, for I am with you; do not be dismayed, for I am your God" (Isaiah 41:10). And he knows that when his pilgrimage comes to an end, "all the trumpets" will be blowing "for him on the other side." (Dr. Siegbert Becker, *The Foolishness of God*, second edition, pages 213-215)

Q: **What is so dangerous about teaching "once saved, always saved"?**

A: Teaching "once saved, always saved" tries to solve logically the previous question by refusing to take seriously any scriptural warnings about falling from faith. It is a doctrine that assumes God must not be quite serious when he said through Paul, "So, if you think you are standing firm, be careful that you don't fall" (1 Corinthians 10:12). Teaching "once saved, always saved" is a dangerous doctrine that creates secure and self-confident believers who may fail to run for shelter to the cross of Christ in the storms of temptation.

10. We reject the false and blasphemous conclusion that those who are lost were predestined, or elected, by God to damnation, for God wants all people to be saved (1 Timothy 2:4; 2 Peter 3:9).

Q: If God chose some to be saved in eternity, why isn't it also reasonable to say that he must have chosen in eternity some to be condemned?

A: For those who are reading this whole book, please forgive the repetition. Is the conclusion above logical? Yes. Is it biblical? No. A teaching that God from eternity wanted some people to be damned paints God as a deceiver who has claimed to be reaching out to the world with Christ when in fact he has never really wanted the whole world to be saved. Such a teaching calls God a liar when he says, "As surely as I live, declares the Sovereign LORD, I take no pleasure in the death of the wicked, but rather that they turn from their ways and live" (Ezekiel 33:11).

> 11. We reject universalism, the belief that all people are saved, even those without faith in Christ (John 3:36). We reject pluralism, the belief that there are other ways to salvation besides faith in Christ (John 14:6; Acts 4:12). We reject any teaching that says it does not matter what one believes so long as one has faith in God.

Q: Isn't the teaching of "universalism" just taking seriously the fact that Jesus made a payment for the sins of the entire world?

A: While "universalism" may take seriously Scripture's statements about the universality of Christ's work, it fails to take seriously Scripture's clear statements about the disastrous results of unbelief. Jesus could hardly speak any more clearly than he does in Mark 16:16: "Whoever believes and is baptized will be saved, but whoever does not believe will be

condemned." The entire conversation of Jesus with Nicode-
mus in John 3 confirms the teaching of the rest of Scripture.

 **Aren't all religions the same? Don't they
teach people of many different cultures about
the one true God, only in different ways and
with different names?**

A: Such a statement sounds good to human ears, but it
ignores the fact that if that were the case, God would be a
grand deceiver who would be saying utterly contradictory
things to people of different cultures. All other world religions
make people their own saviors in order to make themselves
right with God or the gods. Only Christianity offers us a Savior who came to earth to give us what we could not achieve on
our own. Christianity and all other world religions are not relatively compatible branches sprung from the same tree. They
are as different as day and night. That's what Peter told the
Jewish Sanhedrin shortly after Pentecost, and it is still the
truth today: "[Jesus Christ] is 'the stone you builders rejected,
which has become the capstone.' Salvation is found in no one
else, for there is no other name under heaven given to men by
which we must be saved" (Acts 4:11,12).

Claiming that all religions basically teach the same thing is
a teaching designed to win praise from people. However, it is a
lie forged in the fires of hell by Satan, who knows the truth and
trembles (James 2:19).

**Aren't we being arrogant and intolerant to
claim that Jesus is the only right way to salvation?**

A: If the message of the gospel were nothing but a
human story that someone had authored in order to try to make

sense out of our world, we would indeed be arrogant and intolerant to insist that "Jesus is the only right way to salvation." But since the gospel is God's message to his world, the real arrogance and intolerance is to reject God's own message about God's own Son who was sent to be our only Savior. Any other message of salvation is "really no gospel at all" (Galatians 1:7).

Additional Reading for This Section:

The Proper Distinction between Law and Gospel by C. F. W. Walther
Law and Gospel: Foundation of Lutheran Ministry by Robert J. Koester
Law and Gospel: Bad News—Good News by Leroy A. Dobberstein
Predestination: Chosen in Christ by John A. Moldstad, Jr.
Justification: How God Forgives by Wayne D. Mueller
Conversion: Not by My Own Choosing by John M. Brenner
Justification: Am I Good Enough for God? by Rolf Preus

Section V.
GOOD WORKS AND PRAYER

1. We believe that faith in Jesus Christ always leads a believer to produce works that are pleasing to God. "Faith by itself, if it is not accompanied by action, is dead" (James 2:17). As a branch in Christ the vine, a Christian produces good fruit (John 15:5).

 What is a good work?

A good work is something that a believer does (John 15:5) out of love for Christ and his free gift of salvation (2 Corinthians 5:14). A believer desires to follow God's will and to do what agrees with God's holy will (Psalm 119:32). The Scriptures summarize the principles or standards for a believer's good works in the Ten Commandments.

How do we avoid thinking that good works are necessary for salvation if we say that faith "always leads a believer to produce works that are pleasing to God"?

Why does a fruit tree produce fruit? In order to make itself a fruit tree? No. It produces fruit because it is a fruit tree. In fact, if a fruit tree is not producing fruit, it is either dead or dying.

So it is with Christians and their fruits of faith. As Jesus said, "I am the vine; you are the branches. If a man remains in me and I in him, he will bear much fruit" (John 15:5). Because believers are connected to Jesus, they are alive to salvation. As those who are now spiritually alive, it isn't that we believers *might* bear much fruit nor is it that we *must* bear much fruit. Jesus promises that every believer attached to him as the vine "*will* bear much fruit." Such promises of God lead us to say that faith "always leads a believer to produce works that are pleasing to God." The power of the Spirit through the gospel produces faith that shows itself to be alive. A faith that is not living is no real faith. "Faith by itself, if it is not accompanied by action, is dead" (James 2:17). This does not mean that works earn salvation, but fruits of faith are the natural visible evidence that a believer *already* possesses life and salvation in Jesus.

2. We believe that works pleasing to God are works of love, for "love is the fulfillment of the law" (Romans 13:10). Faith, however, does not set up its own standards to determine what is loving (Matthew 15:9). True faith delights to do only what agrees with God's holy will. That will of God is revealed in the Bible, particularly in the Ten Commandments as their content is repeated in the New Testament. In wrestling with current moral problems, the Christian will therefore seek answers from God's law.

Q: Define *love* as it's used here.

A: The apostle Paul provides a beautiful description. He wrote, "Love is patient, love is kind. It does not envy, it does not boast, it is not proud. It is not rude, it is not self-seeking, it is not easily angered, it keeps no record of wrongs. Love does not delight in evil but rejoices with the truth. It always protects, always trusts, always hopes, always perseveres" (1 Corinthians 13:4-7). The description defines *love* by what it does and what it does not do. Love is always seeking to do what is best for others. When a believer loves God, that believer will give God the primary position in his or her life and seek to do what God wants at all times.

The Ten Commandments provide clear directions for loving God and others. As if that were not enough, throughout Scripture God gives many living illustrations in the lives of real people of what love is and what it is not.

Q: Why are God's standards for love more important than setting our own standards?

A: Jesus often dealt with the Pharisees during his earthly ministry. They were fond of setting up their own standards of what it meant to love God and neighbor. At the same time, they ignored genuine love for God and neighbor. By doing this they defined love in whatever way allowed them to live as they wished to live. But Jesus denounced their self-created standard of love. Because their standard ignored real love for God and neighbor, Jesus said, "You hypocrites! Isaiah was right when he prophesied about you: 'These people honor me with their lips, but their hearts are far from me. They worship me in vain; their teachings are but rules taught by men'" (Matthew 15:7-9).

Q: What are we to do about current moral problems or situations that God's law does not seem to address?

A: First, we must remember that the Bible's main purpose is to make us "wise for salvation through faith in Christ Jesus" (2 Timothy 3:15). The Bible was not written with the primary purpose of giving us a complete code of laws and regulations that would give us an easy answer to every decision in life. Such a code of laws and regulations could never save us, even if we sought to devote our whole lives to following its moral precepts.

Nevertheless, it is still amazing how the Bible answers very specific modern moral problems. The Bible gives such answers, not because it mentions every specific moral question that could ever arise in the history of the world but, rather, the Bible presents God's basic principles for what is moral and immoral, defining that which is evil and that which is good. Armed with those basic principles, we are guided to wise decisions as new specific questions arise.

For instance, the Scriptures obviously make no specific reference to many modern life-and-death issues, yet the principle that "The LORD brings death and makes alive" (1 Samuel 2:6) guides us in making decisions. With that principle we consider life a precious gift of God that we should treat with respect.

3. We believe, for example, that the Fifth Commandment teaches that all human life is a gift from God. This commandment speaks against abortion, suicide, and euthanasia ("mercy killing").

Q: Besides the words of the Fifth Commandment, where else does Scripture teach that life is a gift from God?

A: The passage referred to in the previous answer (1 Samuel 2:6) is a powerful reminder that God holds the right both to begin life and to end it. In addition to the Fifth Commandment, other passages include Psalm 31:15: "My times are in your hands." In this passage, the psalmist finds comfort in knowing that every moment of our existence is secure in God's hands. Certainly any list of such passages would be incomplete without noting God's creating activity in Genesis 1 and 2, especially Genesis 2:7: "The LORD God formed the man from the dust of the ground and breathed into his nostrils the breath of life, and the man became a living being."

Q: Is abortion ever the best option?

A: If allowing a pregnancy to continue would result in the death of both mother and child, then an abortion may indeed be necessary to save the life of the mother. Such is the case in an ectopic pregnancy (sometimes called a tubal pregnancy) when the fertilized egg implants itself in the fallopian tube or outside of the uterine cavity.

However, in the case of a pregnancy caused by rape or incest, to sentence the unborn child to death for the sin of the "father" is neither just nor right.

Q: Are there any forms of euthanasia that would not be considered murder?

A: As many typically use the term, all forms of euthanasia are really nothing more than human beings trying to play the role of God in determining who has a right to live and who does not. To play God is arrogant and always a sin. When we play God in matters of life and death, we are committing murder.

We must remember two important truths. First and foremost is that the beginning and end of life are in God's hands. At the same time, we also understand that this does not release us from all responsibility in using our God-given wisdom and knowledge to discern when God clearly seems to be bringing a life to an end. Where death is *not* imminent, we play God and violate the principle that life is in God's hands if we directly cause the death of another. We violate that principle even when we rationalize such action in order to ease pain or because life lacks some subjective "quality" we feel it must have to justify continued existence. At the same time, we can refuse certain medical treatments or discontinue them. For example, if after seeking competent medical advice it appears that death is imminent in a matter of days or hours and medical treatment is only prolonging the process of dying, then refusing or discontinuing certain medical treatment may make a powerful statement that we believe that God holds our times in his hands.

Q: **Since a person who commits suicide doesn't have time to repent of that sin, is there any chance of that individual being saved?**

A: We need to begin by remembering that Christians do not fall from faith every time they sin. If that were true, we would be falling from faith countless times every day since we possess within us a sinful nature that always opposes God. With the apostle Paul, we must confess, "I know that nothing good lives in me, that is, in my sinful nature" (Romans 7:18). While that struggle against our sinful nature continues, we rejoice with Paul that we possess victory in Jesus (verses 24,25).

In other words, while every sin deserves damnation and persisting in refusing to repent of sin destroys faith, wherever saving faith exists we stand in God's grace through Jesus Christ (Romans 5:1,2). Saving faith clings to the perfect life and death of Jesus, not to the perfection of its repentance. Our repentance does not earn God's forgiveness, but repentance is an attitude of heart that hates sin and turns daily to the Savior's grace. Therefore, even in cases where the opportunity to repent of a particular sin may be cut short, that does not mean that a person is lost.

The real question is one of faith or unbelief. Did the person who died by his or her own hand die in faith in Jesus Christ? If a suicide was a premeditated act of despair that utterly rejected God's help in life, it indeed may be evidence of a loss of faith in Jesus. Therefore, the real problem was more than no time to repent. Did the person who committed suicide abandon God's help and reject his promises? If that was true, then the suicide reveals an impenitent heart that rejected all the love and grace of God.

On the other hand, if a suicide was a rash act of momentary weakness or of confusion of a mind under great pressure, it is very possible that saving faith in Christ may not have been extinguished. If the person was standing through faith in the grace of God, despite the fact that there was no time for repentance, that person still stands in the righteousness of Christ as a child of God.

Of course, only God can see the existence of saving faith or the lack of it; we are limited to drawing conclusions from what we see and hear. No one, simple answer can be given about whether someone who has committed suicide has gone to heaven or hell. Indeed, our most pressing concern should not be trying to peer into eternity but rather to seek out those who may be discouraged or depressed to remind them of the grace of God in Jesus Christ.

Q: If life is God's gift, can we carry out the death penalty?

A: Scripture clearly proclaims the truth that the beginning and end of life are in God's hands: "The LORD brings death and makes alive; he brings down to the grave and raises up" (1 Samuel 2:6). Life is God's gift, and only he has the authority to bring it to an end.

However, God often exercises some of his authority through human beings. God maintains law and order through the government, "which God has established" (Romans 13:1). Someone serving in government "is God's servant to do you good. But if you do wrong, be afraid, for he does not bear the sword for nothing. He is God's servant, an agent of wrath to bring punishment on the wrongdoer" (Romans 13:4). It is significant that Paul mentions the "sword" as a symbol for the government's God-given authority against those who do wrong. The sword was one mode of execution used by the Roman government. When a government acts justly against someone who has committed a serious crime, it is not violating God's gift of life. Rather, the government is acting as God's servant, exercising the authority over life God gave.

4. We believe that the Sixth Commandment regulates marriage and the family. God instituted marriage as a life-long union of one man and one woman (Matthew 19:4-6). It is the only proper context for sexual intimacy and the procreation of children. A marriage can be ended without sin only when God ends the marriage through the death of one of the spouses. Nevertheless, a Christian may obtain a divorce if his or her spouse has broken the marriage through adultery (Matthew 19:9) or malicious desertion (1 Corinthians 7:15). The Sixth Commandment forbids all sexual intimacy apart from marriage, including homosexuality (1 Corinthians 6:9,10).

Is there anywhere besides Matthew 19 where Scripture teaches that marriage is defined as being between one man and one woman?

A: The best place to go would be to the account of the creation of Adam and Eve in Genesis 2. When God established marriage, he created one man and then one woman to be "a helper suitable for him" (Genesis 2:18). It is very significant that Jesus quotes from Genesis 2 in his discussion of marriage in Matthew 19. When Jesus seeks to illustrate for us what God intends marriage to be, he goes back to that beginning in the Garden of Eden. It is also significant that nowhere does Scripture depict in a positive light any kind of sexual relationship between those of the same sex.

Q: Some say that the Bible isn't forbidding all homosexual relationships, just promiscuous abuses of sexuality, such as homosexual prostitution. Is that true?

A: Such arguments are nothing more than the common instinct of our sinful human nature to try to defend and excuse its sin. The apostle Paul uses strong language in Romans 1:26,27: "Because of this, God gave them over to shameful lusts. Even their women exchanged natural relations for unnatural ones. In the same way the men also abandoned natural relations with women and were inflamed with lust for one another. Men committed indecent acts with other men, and received in themselves the due penalty for their perversion." Paul describes sexual intimacy between people of the same sex as "unnatural," "indecent," and "perversion." Paul isn't just speaking about promiscuous homosexual sexual relations. Instead, any sexual contact between persons of the same sex is a distortion of God's gifts of male and female. In fact, if you look at the whole context of

Romans 1, such sexual perversion is a result of utterly shutting out the true knowledge of God.

Q: **Why would we disapprove of a lifelong, faithful union between two men or two women?**

A: Please read again the simple and clear statement of Paul from Romans 1 quoted in the answer to the previous question. The question is not whether a homosexual relationship is faithful or promiscuous; the question is whether any such relationship is pleasing to God at all. The direction God gives us in Scripture is clear. A lifelong, faithful union of two men or two women twists and perverts God's plan for male and female. That this is clearly the case cannot be denied by those who listen to Scripture rather than their own reason.

Q: **Why did God restrict sexual intimacy to marriage?**

A: Nowhere does God have a specific list of his reasons to limit sexual intimacy to marriage, though it is clear from Scripture that he does. Hebrews 13:4 clearly reminds us, "Marriage should be honored by all, and the marriage bed kept pure, for God will judge the adulterer and all the sexually immoral."

While God has not furnished us with an exhaustive list of why he has reserved sexual intimacy for marriage, we can learn at least one reason by taking a look at God's institution of marriage. Marriage is the most intimate human relationship God designed for this world. When God brought Eve to Adam and established marriage, the Scriptures say, "For this reason a man will leave his father and mother and be united to his wife, and they will become one flesh" (Genesis 2:24).

Marriage assumes that all other human relationships come secondary, even that of parent and child. It also assumes that two people openly and freely commit their lives to each other in a lifelong relationship. As one man and one woman unite themselves to each other, then, and only then, do two people become "one flesh." Those words indicate more than just sexual intimacy—God intended an entire interweaving of the lives of husband and wife. Yet sexual relations are the most intimate expressions of that "one flesh" life together in marriage. When two people commit their lives to each other and are united as husband and wife, their sexual intimacy is truly the selfless giving to each other that God intended it to be.

Outside of marriage, physical intimacy asks for a physical expression without the commitment of a full and lifelong relationship. Instead of being an expression of such a whole commitment to another in every way, sexual intimacy outside of marriage becomes a taking of sexual pleasure without any commitment. Sexual intimacy outside of marriage is nothing more than the union of two bodies rather than two lives. Such a distortion of God's plan violates his beautiful gift of marriage and its true "one flesh" relationship. God did not create us to selfishly use others for as long as they give us pleasure, even if such selfish pleasure is mutually consented by adults.

God also intended marriage for the purpose of bringing children into his world. He told Adam and Eve, "Be fruitful and increase in number" (Genesis 1:28). God desired to bless each child with a loving father and mother who are committed to raising their child in a home in which they live together as husband and wife. Our sinful nature sometimes distorts and fractures the environment of a loving home with two parents and children. Nevertheless, such a home is God's ideal environment for the growth and development of children. God said, "Has not the LORD made them one? In flesh and spirit they are his. And why one? Because he was seeking godly offspring" (Malachi 2:15).

Q: How can we say homosexuality is wrong when it appears some people may be born with such an inclination?

A: No unbiased, conclusive medical study confirms homosexuality is an inborn disposition. Even if such studies did conclusively show a biological component to homosexuality, that still would not make it right. We know we are all born with a sinful nature that is dead in sin and hostile to God. As Jesus reminds us in Matthew 15:19, many things flow quite "naturally" out of our natural sinful hearts: "evil thoughts, murder, adultery, sexual immorality, theft, false testimony, slander." We don't defend such sins because they come to us naturally. Rather, we flee to the cross of Jesus for forgiveness and for power to run from such temptations. The same should be true with any "natural," or "biological," inclination to homosexuality.

Q: Why are we concerned about a man-made institution that requires a piece of paper by the government?

A: A quick reading of Genesis 2 or Matthew 19 reveals clearly that marriage is not a man-made institution, but God established and instituted marriage.

It is true that God has not demanded that governments establish marriage laws, such as requiring a marriage license. Yet the government is within its God-given authority to regulate marriage for the purpose of keeping good order in society. The government has an interest in passing laws that help society understand clearly who is married and who is not. Such laws help protect family inheritance and property as well as protect children and spouses from being forsaken by those who ignore their responsibilities. For a Christian to ignore governmental laws concerning marriage is to violate the Fourth Commandment as well as to give offense by seeming to treat marriage more lightly than even unbelievers in society.

Q: For what reasons can a marriage be dissolved in divorce?

A: God gave Adam and Eve to each other and intended that their relationship be not only intimate and sexual but also endure throughout their lives. Jesus responded to the same question with these words, "I tell you that anyone who divorces his wife, except for marital unfaithfulness, and marries another woman commits adultery" (Matthew 19:9). Sexual unfaithfulness dissolves the intimate relationship of marriage implied by the "one flesh" of Genesis 2:24. The apostle Paul provided another reason for divorce. He wrote, "If the unbeliever leaves, let him do so. A believing man or woman is not bound in such circumstances; God has called us to live in peace" (1 Corinthians 7:15). Desertion is clearly another way in which the marriage is destroyed. In other cases, husband and wife will find ways to solve problems and difficulties and keep the marriage bond. Divorce recognizes the end of the union. Where sexual unfaithfulness and desertion have not destroyed the relationships, believers will seek God's help and consult counselors for solutions rather than end their marriages.

Q: Would physical or emotional abuse ever be the same as "malicious desertion"?

A: First, a word of caution: Some eagerly look for a supposed biblical reason as an excuse to end a marriage because they are dissatisfied. They have not been deserted but, in fact, are in danger of being the ones deserting the marriage. When

Paul mentions "such circumstances" in 1 Corinthians 7:15 (see previous answer), he indicates that he is speaking about a category of actions that destroy marriages. The category is made up of actions on the part of one spouse that make it impossible for the other spouse to live in peace. For example, physical abuse by which the health and even life of the spouse or a child are in danger can indeed make life together impossible. God has given us not only the Sixth Commandment but also the Fifth Commandment. To continue to put life and health in danger would violate the Fifth Commandment. Certainly, in all "such circumstances," a Christian spouse would seek ways to change the circumstances before the marriage would need to be dissolved.

It is also conceivable that a spouse's sinful hatred could show itself in such severe verbal and emotional cruelty that life together in peace would be impossible. But also in those circumstances, the spouse should seek the counsel and advice of other Christians who value God's gift of marriage to see if there is another way to deal with such unloving behavior.

5. We believe that individuals are free to make their own decisions concerning matters that are neither forbidden nor commanded by God's Word (adiaphora). People must be careful, however, that their use of this freedom does not cause others to sin.

Q: **What does it mean to be "careful" about using our Christian freedom?**

A: The apostle Paul reminds us in Romans 14:13 why we should be "careful" about using our freedom: "Make up your mind not to put any stumbling block or obstacle in your brother's way." For example, I may be able to make use of alcohol without stumbling to the abuse of drunkenness. But there may be a fellow Christian for whom taking even one alcoholic beverage would mean not stopping until he or she was drunk, plunging his or her life back into alcoholism. When I am with that fellow Christian, it would be an unloving abuse of my freedom to exercise my ability to use alcohol when that may be an overwhelming temptation to my brother or sister to abuse it. His or her well-being is far more important at that moment than having an alcoholic beverage. My freedom to drink may encourage the downward spiral of alcoholism. My abuse of my freedom may send my brother or sister in faith on a course that jeopardizes his or her faith.

Q: **Are there times when we might purposefully make use of our freedom to make a point about the truth of the gospel?**

A: At times others may try to bind our freedom by telling us that we are sinning by a particular action when God has not labeled it as sinful. At such times, we may need to give testimony to our gospel freedom by doing that which God permits but these others forbid. For example, there are some Christian denominations that insist that Baptism can only be done by completely immersing in water the one who is being baptized. While immersion can indeed be a beautiful symbol of the death and resurrection that the Holy Spirit accomplishes in our baptism, nowhere does Scripture ever command a certain method of applying the water in Baptism. Therefore, one of the reasons our Lutheran church pours the water instead of immersing is to declare clearly that Baptism is pure gospel and not some legal ordinance in which the water must be applied in a certain way to be legitimate.

6. We believe that good works, which are fruits of faith, must be distinguished from works of civic righteousness performed by unbelievers. Although unbelievers may do much that appears to be good and upright, these works are not good in God's sight, for "without faith it is impossible to please God" (Hebrews 11:6). While we recognize the value of such works for human society, we know that unbelievers cannot do their duty to God through works of civic righteousness.

 If an unbeliever's acts of civic righteousness are not good in God's sight, why don't we discourage them?

A: Good citizenship, truth, integrity, honor, diligence, faithfulness, concern for the unfortunate, environmental responsibility, and other virtues benefit all of society and should be honored and encouraged. We praise acts of civic righteousness performed by unbelievers as long as our praise gives no indication that such acts improve their standing in the sight of God. However, if we praise acts of civic righteousness in such a way that people become proud, as if their actions render unnecessary a Savior and his life and death for them, then we have done a great disservice to the gospel and have created nothing but proud Pharisees. We are not trying to discourage actions that benefit society. What we are trying to discourage is proud spiritual arrogance that blinds people to their need for Jesus.

Q: **How is it fair to say that a believer and an unbeliever can carry out the same outward act of kindness or compassion and for one it would be a good work and for another it would not be?**

A: Before God the forgiveness of sins is most important. He sent his Son, Jesus, to cleanse us of all sin. A believer's works are cleansed of every stain of sin through Jesus (1 John 1:7). An unbeliever has no forgiveness, because he or she has not accepted God's forgiveness by faith in Jesus. Works produced by believers and unbelievers may be very similar on the outside, but the believer's acts come from a heart and a mind that know Jesus and his forgiveness. What delights God are hearts that render service to him or to a fellow human being because they are moved by his love and reflect his grace. Without faith in Jesus the motives of the heart behind outwardly good actions have no sense of serving Jesus. Even when the works are motivated by a sincere desire to help others, we abide by the verdict of Jesus. He said that apart from him we "can do nothing" (John 15:5).

7. We believe that in this world even the best works of Christians are tainted with sin. A sinful nature still afflicts every Christian. Therefore Christians often fail to do the good they want to do but keep on doing the evil they do not want to do (Romans 7:18-21). They must confess that all their righteous acts are like filthy rags (Isaiah 64:6). Because of Christ's redemption, however, these imperfect efforts of Christians are considered holy and acceptable by their heavenly Father.

Q: Won't teaching that all our best works are tainted with sin discourage Christians from living for Christ?

A: Scripture also teaches that our good works are pleasing in God's sight because even their imperfections stand under the forgiving grace of Christ. Again and again the Scriptures encourage us to live active Christian lives of service to God and others. But that does not take away the fact that Scripture clearly teaches, "All of us have become like one who is unclean, and all our righteous acts are like filthy rags" (Isaiah 64:6). If such is the confession of the prophet Isaiah and the people of God of Isaiah's day, can anything less be said about us? This biblical teaching that our good works are tainted by sin is an antidote to our tendency to be proud of our efforts rather than to focus on our Savior and his forgiveness.

Q: **Where in Scripture is it taught that God accepts our imperfect works as perfectly pleasing in his sight for Jesus' sake?**

A: When Jesus speaks about the sheep, or believers, on his right on judgment day, he commends them for the evidence of their faith (see Matthew 25:31-46). He makes no comments about any of their sins or even the imperfections of those very fruits of faith. The imperfections and all the rest of their sins have already been forgiven. They are removed from them "as far as the east is from the west" (Psalm 103:12). Since all sin is forgiven and paid for in the life and death of Jesus, all that is left for God to see in our good works is their good.

8. We believe that the Holy Spirit enables every believer to produce good works as fruits of faith (Galatians 5:22-25). The Holy Spirit gives every believer a new nature, or "new man," that cooperates with the Holy Spirit in doing good works. The Holy Spirit uses the gospel to motivate believers to do good works.

Q: **Why do we say here that we cooperate with the Holy Spirit in our good works but not in our conversion?**

A: If we teach that there is some spiritual cooperation before we are brought to faith, that would be false doctrine. Before we are brought to faith, we are dead in sin (Ephesians 2:1) and hostile to God (Romans 8:7). We can't cooperate with God in the least. But in the water of our baptism, we are buried with Christ and rise to live with Christ (see Romans 6:1-4). When we are brought to faith, God plants a new self within us. Paul describes that new self as being "created to be like God in true righteousness and holiness" (Ephesians 4:24). That new self, created by the Spirit himself, possesses the power to cooperate with the Holy Spirit in producing fruits of faith.

Q: How does the Holy Spirit use the gospel to "motivate believers to do good works"?

A: The power of God's love for us in Jesus Christ works in us both to have the desire and to have the power to carry out good works in our lives. Whenever we hear or remember the gospel of Jesus in Word and sacrament, we are filled both with a desire to live a thankful life and the power to do so. As Paul tells us in Philippians 2:13, "It is God who works in you to will and to act according to his good purpose."

9. The Holy Spirit also equips the church with all the spiritual gifts it needs for its well-being (1 Corinthians 12:4-11). During the beginning of the New Testament era, special charismatic gifts were given to the church, such as signs, miracles, and speaking in tongues. These gifts were connected with the ministry of the apostles (2 Corinthians 12:12). There is no evidence in Scripture that we today should expect the continuation of such charismatic gifts.

What kinds of spiritual gifts does the Spirit give to the church?

A: Nowhere in Scripture does God give us an exhaustive list of such gifts. However, if you read through Romans 12, 1 Corinthians 12, and 1 Peter 4, you will find a rather lengthy list of the many spiritual gifts that the Holy Spirit showers on his people. These gifts are given to God's people in order to meet the particular needs of the ministry of the gospel in every age. Sometimes Bible students divide the Spirit's gifts into serving gifts and speaking gifts. But perhaps the most important truth to keep in mind is that the Holy Spirit gives to each believer the precise spiritual gifts he or she needs to carry out the service of the gospel God has planned. In 1 Corinthians 12:7, Paul assures us that "to each one the manifestation of the Spirit is given for the common good." These gifts are indeed given to "each one" so that we might accomplish the "good works, which God prepared in advance for us to do" (Ephesians 2:10).

Q: **What does Scripture mean when it mentions "speaking in tongues"?**

A: The clearest example of "speaking in tongues" in the Scriptures is in Acts 2 on the day of Pentecost. At Pentecost, speaking in tongues was clearly the miraculous ability to speak in known human languages. The disciples did not have a speaking knowledge of those languages, but the Holy Spirit gave them that miraculous ability. The response of the hearers in Acts 2:5-11 confirms that definition. They suddenly heard the gospel proclaimed in their native languages. It is enlightening to note that the Greek word that is used for this miracle of the Holy Spirit is also the regular Greek word for "languages."

All other references to speaking in tongues are relatively brief scriptural references. Acts 2 indicates that speaking in tongues may have always been the ability to speak known human languages for the advancement of the gospel. Nevertheless, a brief comment in 1 Corinthians 13:1 ("If I speak in the tongues of men and of angels, but have not love . . .") may indicate that it is possible that at times speaking in tongues could also have meant speaking in a language otherwise unknown.

 Why did the Holy Spirit give to the early Christian church such miraculous outward gifts such as healing and speaking in tongues?

A: While God can do miracles anywhere and anytime he pleases, if you look back at recorded Bible history stretching from the Garden of Eden until the time of the apostles, you will notice that God has not typically used flurries of miracles to accomplish the work of his kingdom. God's typical course of action is to accomplish wonders in human hearts through the quiet whisper of his gospel message shared from heart to heart by human messengers.

Yet at certain crucial times in his plan of salvation, he has permitted a significant grouping of miracles. Those times include when he rescued Israel from Egypt, the time when Baal worship had almost extinguished the true knowledge of God during the ministries of Elijah and Elisha, and finally when God was establishing his New Testament church during the ministry of Jesus and the apostles. In those moments of church history, God used special miraculous gifts to support and validate the words of his chosen spokespeople.

Should we expect such special outward gifts today? Are we setting limits on what the Holy Spirit can still do?

A: We certainly cannot limit what God can or cannot do. "Our God is in heaven; he does whatever pleases him" (Psalm 115:3). God can demonstrate his power by miraculous gifts, but he has not promised to do so. God makes it clear to us in the Scriptures what he promises to do, but beyond that we have no promise that God will do anything miraculous. We seek to discern from Scripture what God tells us he has done and what he continues to do.

Nowhere can anyone point to a Scripture verse that indicates that God has promised that every Christian will perform miracles or receive other miraculous spiritual gifts such as speaking in tongues. The danger is not only to say less than Scripture says about such gifts but also to say more than it says. In 1 Corinthians 12:29-31, the apostle Paul makes it very clear that God has not made a blanket promise of such gifts to all Christians. In fact, in those same verses, Paul values those more outwardly astounding gifts as less than God's greater spiritual gifts of faith, hope, and love. Some Christian groups within the visible church (often called pentecostal or charismatic) claim, without justification from Scripture, that all true Christians should expect such special outpouring of spiritual gifts. They claim such miraculous gifts are a mark of advancement in the kingdom of God. It is also interesting to note what Jesus said to those in his day who repeatedly demanded from him just such miraculous signs: "A wicked and adulterous generation looks for a miraculous sign" (Matthew 16:4).

Scripture provides us with a better approach. While the New Testament was being written and established as the inspired Word of God, God confirmed the truth and reliability of the Word of his apostles by granting them some very spectacular spiritual gifts. The need for such gifts is not the same today since we have the complete apostolic New Testament Scriptures.

One last thought is very important. Those who typically claim that we, as Lutherans, do not value the gifts of the Spirit are the same ones who often refuse to see that the Spirit truly works through the gospel in Word and sacrament (the means of grace). They tend to scoff at his gift of Baptism as nothing but water. They refuse to see him at work in the Lord's Supper, in the simple bread and wine connected with Jesus' real body and blood. They refuse to see that the Holy Spirit deserves all the credit for bringing believers to faith. Instead they depend on a human decision or a human inclination or feeling. Isn't it fair to ask who really is downplaying the most important work of the Holy Spirit? Is it those who are skeptical about some claims of speaking in tongues and doing miracles or those who are skeptical about the very means of grace by which the Holy Spirit does his most vital work of creating and strengthening faith?

10. We believe that a life of prayer is a fruit of faith. Confidently, through faith in their Savior, Christians address their heavenly Father with petitions and praise. They present their needs and the needs of others, and they give thanks (1 Timothy 2:1). Such prayers are a delight to God, and he grants their requests according to his wisdom (Matthew 7:7,8; 1 John 5:14).

Q: What is meant by the phrase "life of prayer"?

A: When the apostle Paul urges us to "pray continually" (1 Thessalonians 5:17), he clearly doesn't mean that we must always be found with our heads bowed, hands folded, and eyes closed. But he does mean that we should be quick to speak to our heavenly Father in thanksgiving about every need of life for ourselves and all others at all times. A "life of prayer" is that continual conversation that beloved children of God carry on as they address their dear heavenly Father. Prayer is the natural response of the children of God who know that because of the life, death, and resurrection of our Lord Jesus, they can approach God at any time, for anything, and for anyone. Believers rely on God's promise that their prayers will never be turned aside. As Paul puts it, "In him and through faith in him we may approach God with freedom and confidence" (Ephesians 3:12).

Remember that the second half of this conversation occurs as we listen carefully to God's response to us in the Word and sacrament.

Q : **Scripture has some bold statements about us receiving whatever we ask for in prayer. Does God really promise to fulfill those open-ended promises?**

A : We are to take such promises of God at full face value. Of course, children of God would never presume to remove from their heavenly Father the freedom to improve upon the answers he gives to our prayers. Where sinful selfishness or spiritual near-sightedness causes us to ask for what would truly be harmful to others or ourselves, we trust our heavenly Father to improve upon our prayers and grant us what is even better than what we have asked. That is what we mean when we say that we trust that God answers our prayers "according to his wisdom." John puts that into simple form when he writes in his first epistle, "This is the confidence we have in approaching God: that if we ask anything according to his will, he hears us. And if we know that he hears us— whatever we ask—we know that we have what we asked of him" (1 John 5:14,15). Notice how John took at full face value God's promise to hear and answer every prayer. At the same time, he also cautioned believers to defer exact answers to the gracious and loving will of the Father. Without that understanding, prayer would become nothing more than the demands of spoiled children, stomping their feet until their father concedes to their demands. A view of prayer that refuses to allow room for God's will and timing in his answers really reverses the roles of who is God and who is the child.

Q: Why do our prayers delight God?

A: The prayers of God's children in Jesus delight him because we are taking him at his promises and living by them. In Psalm 50:15 God proclaims to us, "Call upon me in the day of trouble; I will deliver you, and you will honor me." The mere acts of believing God's promise to hear us in trouble and running to him in prayer honor him. Whenever believers turn their eyes heavenward to thank God for blessings or seek future blessings for themselves or others, they make a powerful statement that they trust not in themselves but in their gracious God and his wonderful promises. God delights, therefore, in our prayers because they boldly proclaim before the world that we have taken to heart his promises: "Trust in the LORD with all your heart and lean not on your own understanding; in all your ways acknowledge him, and he will make your paths straight" (Proverbs 3:5,6).

Q: Should we be praying to God in general, or is it better to address our prayers to a specific person of the triune God?

A: As long as we are coming in faith to the one true and triune God, it does not matter whether we say "God" or speak the prayer more specifically to any one of the three persons of the Godhead. Since all three persons are coequal and coeternal, we are approaching the God in whom we trust whether we say "Jesus," "Father," or "Holy Spirit" in our prayers.

 You often hear people asking their pastor to pray for them. Are we to understand that his prayers are more powerful or effective than ours?

A: There is nothing wrong with asking another Christian, including a pastor, to pray for us. Scripture urges us to pray for one another in our needs in life (James 5:16). One person's prayer is not more valuable or powerful than another's. In Christ we are all equal before God. Believers do not pray on the basis of their own righteousness or goodness but on the basis of Christ alone. Everyone whose trust is in Jesus Christ has the same power of prayer as anyone else whose trust is in him.

James makes that point powerfully as he compares each of us to the prophet Elijah. "Elijah was a man just like us. He prayed earnestly that it would not rain, and it did not rain on the land for three and a half years. Again he prayed, and the heavens gave rain, and the earth produced its crops" (James 5:17,18). James reminds us that "Elijah was a man just like us." Since everyone who believes in Jesus Christ is a child of God who has been washed and declared righteous in the blood of Christ, we all have the same access to God's throne of grace! The prayers of all such sinners declared righteous in Christ are indeed "powerful and effective" (James 5:16).

11. We reject every thought that the good works of Christians in any way earn or contribute toward establishing a right relationship with God and gaining salvation in heaven.

Q: Why do we so strongly reject any thought of our good works contributing to a right relationship with God?

A: We strongly reject any contribution of good works to our salvation because that would destroy any possibility of our being saved. To mix our obedience with Christ's obedience in our place is an eternally foolish attempt to produce salvation that is partially by God and partially by us. By doing so, we are trying to find our salvation in law instead of gospel.

The Scriptures strongly reject such a thought. The apostle Paul speaks strong words to those who wish to have their works play even a small part in their salvation: "You who are trying to be justified by law have been alienated from Christ; you have fallen away from grace" (Galatians 5:4). Paul didn't write those words to Pharisees who were completely rejecting Christ but to members of a Christian congregation who were trying to add a few works of law to the work of Christ. To add human works to Christ's completed work places humans back under the impossible burden of perfect and complete obedience to the law. There are only two ways of salvation: trusting fully in the work of Christ or depending fully on keeping the law. No one will be saved by the second way.

Q: Since the Scriptures often show God pouring out blessings on obedience to his will, how can we say that our good works don't contribute toward a right relationship with God?

A: When Jesus bowed his head and died on Good Friday, he said something extremely important. "It is finished" (John 19:30), he cried. With those words he let us know that everything that needed to be done for heaven to be ours had been done. To put our trust in our works to make us right with God is to disagree with Jesus, as if he were mistaken on Good Friday. While God does delight in the good works of his children because of Jesus, our works are fruits of faith that spring from our position as loved children of God. They are not what has made God love us. God does bless obedience to his will in many ways. He does that to encourage us to live for him and to accomplish his will in this world. But the good works of a Christian do not change his or her relationship with God. God's love is not influenced by any human effort.

---

12. We reject every attempt to abolish the unchanging moral law of God as revealed in the Bible as the absolute standard of what is right and wrong.

Q: **Is it true that all moral laws are nothing but tools by which one group in society exercises its authority over other groups who are less powerful?**

A: At times people have abused their power to inflict upon others values that they claimed were "right" and "wrong" only to protect their own power and authority. Yet God's absolute standard of right and wrong for human behavior has existed since creation. His standard does not reflect a human thirst for power and authority. Instead it guides our attitudes and actions toward him as our Creator and toward our neighbor. That perfect and unchanging standard of right and wrong is reflected—even in a fallen world—in the voice of conscience that is within us all. That same standard is perfectly summarized in the Ten Commandments, which God wrote in stone at Mount Sinai. This moral standard has remained unchanged and unaltered by the passing of centuries and the changing of the nations and people in power. Humanity can try to ignore this standard or try to silence conscience and claim this standard doesn't exist, but on the basis of this unchanging standard of God's law, all people who have ever lived will be "held accountable to God" (Romans 3:19).

13. We reject the view that people may decide for themselves what is right and wrong apart from God's Word. We reject any misuse of the term *love* to condone behavior contrary to God's Word. We recognize these arguments as schemes of Satan to obscure the knowledge of God's holy will and to undermine the consciousness of sin.

Q: How can we say that we have freedom in many decisions (adiaphora) and at the same time say that we can't decide if anything is right or wrong apart from God's Word?

A: There are many areas of human life that God has clearly indicated as right and wrong. But many decisions of life must be made in areas where God's Word has not established whether one choice is sin and the other is not. For example, each person must choose among many possible careers in life. God has not provided a definite answer. As long as the careers are not essentially evil or dishonest, there is no right or wrong decision. God has left that choice up to each individual. While Christians will certainly pray for wisdom when making such important decisions, they do not have to bear the burden of a troubled conscience as if they were going against God's will by the choices that they make.

Q: Since God has given us the power to think, why shouldn't we be using this power to decide what is loving and what isn't?

A: Certainly there are many times in life when we need to think through a decision and choose what action is loving and what is not. But one cannot abandon what God has revealed in the Scripture. Whenever our intellect would lead us to determine that something is "loving" which God has clearly labeled "sin," we yield to God's definition. He is wiser than we are. Our sinful human nature can easily mislead us. As the prophet Jeremiah warns us, "The heart is deceitful above all things and beyond cure. Who can understand it?" (Jeremiah 17:9). It is because of the deceitfulness of our sinful hearts that we run to God's errorless Word for a clear definition of what love truly is.

14. We reject any view that considers the act of praying a means of grace. Although God certainly gives good gifts to believers in answer to their prayers, he conveys his forgiving grace and strengthens faith only through the Word and sacraments. Furthermore, we reject any view that looks upon prayer as beneficial only because it helps the one who prays feel better.

Q: Explain what it means that prayer is not a means of grace.

A: The direction of prayer is from us to God. Prayer is the privilege that God has given us to communicate to him our thanks and praise and our needs and concerns for ourselves and all others. Scripture does not promise that God will strengthen our faith or increase our knowledge through prayer. God does promise that he will do that through the means of grace, the gospel in Word and sacrament. Through the gospel, God, the Holy Spirit, comes to us and gives us faith, strength, comfort, and knowledge. Prayer by itself is only half of our communication with God. The other half is God's communication with us through the Scriptures. Prayer and study of the Word make for a beautiful two-way communication with God by which we speak to him and he comes to us.

To put it another way, "faith comes from hearing the message" (Romans 10:17) and not from our prayers. That is why we don't direct unbelievers to prayer in order for them to find the Savior; we simply proclaim the truth of the Savior so that the Holy Spirit may work faith in their hearts. Prayer is a fruit that springs from faith. Faith does not spring from prayer.

Q: **What error are we trying to avoid by saying that "we reject any view that looks upon prayer as beneficial only because it helps the one who prays feel better"?**

A: Some do not believe that prayer has any real power or that the true God actually hears and answers prayers. They teach that prayer is beneficial merely because we feel better when we unburden ourselves by going through the motions of prayer. Prayer for them is simply a psychological release or aid. While it is true that prayer brings a psychological relief, that is not the primary reason we pray. We are convinced that the greatest comfort of prayer is knowing that we have a promise from Jesus: "Ask and it will be given to you; seek and you will find; knock and the door will be opened to you" (Matthew 7:7).

15. We reject the view that all prayers are acceptable to God, and we hold that the prayers of all who do not have faith in Christ are vain babbling addressed to false gods (Matthew 6:7).

Q: **What should we think about prayers that are purposefully worded to leave out the name of Jesus so as to not offend those in a group who may not believe in him?**

A: Jesus himself declared, "I am the way and the truth and the life. No one comes to the Father except through me" (John 14:6). To intentionally leave Jesus' name out of a prayer is to give the false impression that there is more than one way to be right with the true God. To participate in such prayers is to value the praise of human beings more highly than praise from God. At such times we need to remember these sobering words of our Lord Jesus, "If anyone is ashamed of me and my words in this adulterous and sinful generation, the Son of Man will be ashamed of him when he comes in his Father's glory with the holy angels" (Mark 8:38). On the Last Day, Jesus will acknowledge every Christian as his child and an heir of heaven. No Christian will be ashamed to declare Jesus "Savior" and "Brother." Christians have no reason to be ashamed of Jesus now. Even if the world wants nothing to do with Christians because they pray to Jesus, believers seek the approval of Jesus rather than the approval of others.

Q: **When might the prayers of Christians become vain babbling?**

A: Whenever our prayers become just so much the mere repetition of words spoken with little or no thought, then we are offering to God nothing more than the vain babbling of the unbelievers. Martin Luther once said that the Lord's Prayer may be the greatest martyr in the world for all of its abuse by Christians who recite it mindlessly.

We are also guilty of vain babbling whenever we speak our prayers but give in to the doubts of our sinful nature. Prayers become vain babbling when we believe that our prayers will not really be heard or answered. At such times James reminds us, "But when he asks, he must believe and not doubt, because he who doubts is like a wave of the sea, blown and tossed by the wind. That man should not think he will receive anything from the Lord; he is a double-minded man, unstable in all he does" (1:6-8). At such times when we feel the doubts that our sinful nature raises, we need to speak the prayer of a man who also wrestled with doubts about God's power to help: "I do believe; help me overcome my unbelief!" (Mark 9:24).

Q: **Would we include the praying of the Roman Catholic rosary as nothing more than "vain babbling addressed to false gods"?**

A: The Roman Catholic rosary is made up of multiple repetitions of the Lord's Prayer interspersed with repetitions of a prayer to the virgin Mary. The constant repetition of the Lord's Prayer seems to have at its heart an idea that God must somehow be persuaded to be merciful by the constant repetition of the same words. While Scripture does indeed urge us to be persistent in our praying as we "cry out to him day and night" (Luke 18:7), to repeat the same words over and over gives the unbiblical impression that God does not delight to answer our prayers but must be worn down by our "many words" (Matthew 6:7).

The inclusion of prayers to Mary together with the Lord's Prayer makes the rosary worse than mere "vain babbling." While there is nothing wrong with asking other living Christians to pray for us, the very words of the prayer to Mary indicate that she is being addressed as though she were our mediator before the throne of God. Roman Catholics believe that prayers to Mary gain special favor and more intimate access to God. The Scriptures say, however, that only Jesus Christ is our mediator who makes our prayers acceptable and powerful in God's sight. "For there is one God and one mediator between God and men, the man Christ Jesus" (1 Timothy 2:5). Prayers to Mary are built on the faulty assumption that she has some special position with God that we do not have. Scripture pictures Mary as a sinner like us who rejoices that she has a Savior. In her beautiful song, called the Magnificat, Mary declares, "My spirit rejoices in God my Savior" (Luke 1:47). Every Christian whose trust is in Jesus Christ has the same access to the throne of grace as any other believer has ever had—including the one believer whom God used to be the human mother of the Savior.

Q: Why don't we pray to the saints in heaven so that they might also speak to God on our behalf? How is that any different than asking a fellow Christian to pray for us?

A: There is no example or command anywhere in Scripture of living believers appealing to dead believers to pray for them. In fact, there is strong indication in Scripture that those who have gone home to heaven before us are ignorant of the details of the world they have left behind. In the book of Isaiah, the prophet directs the Israelites not to their long-dead ancestors—the patriarchs Abraham and Israel—but to the Lord alone. "But you [LORD] are our Father, though Abraham does not know us or Israel acknowledge us; you, O LORD, are our Father, our Redeemer from of old is your name" (Isaiah 63:16). We need no extra advocates in heaven other than our triune God, who has proclaimed through his eternal Son that we are his dearly loved children who have his ear. He hears our prayers at all times.

Additional Reading for This Section:

Prayer: An Audience with the King by Joel V. Petermann

Sanctification: Alive in Christ by Lyle W. Lange

Christian Freedom: Christ Sets Us Free by William E. Fischer

Sanctification: Christ in Action by Harold L. Senkbeil

Luther and Prayer by Martin E. Lehmann

A Simple Way to Pray by Martin Luther (translated by C. J. Trapp)

The Pentecostals and Charismatics: A Confessional Lutheran Evaluation by Arthur J. Clement

Growing Together in Christ by Gene Gronholz and Mark Zarling

Section VI.
THE MEANS OF GRACE

1. We believe that God bestows all spiritual blessings upon sinners by special means established by him. These are the means of grace, the gospel in Word and sacraments. We define a sacrament as a sacred act established by Christ in which the Word connected with an earthly element gives the forgiveness of sins.

Q: Why doesn't God deal with us directly instead of using the means of grace?

A: Since "nothing is impossible with God" (Luke 1:37), there is no doubt that God could have chosen to deal with us directly, without any outward means at all. But what God could do and what he has promised to do are two different things. Nowhere do we have any promise from God that he will speak to our hearts directly, apart from the outward means of the gospel in Word and sacrament. But we have plenty of promises in Scripture that the Holy Spirit works faith and strengthens faith through the outward means that he himself has ordained for our salvation. The Scripture clearly binds us to the proclamation of the gospel when it says, "How, then, can they call on the one they have not believed in? And how can they believe in the one of whom they have not heard? And how can they hear without someone preaching to them? Consequently, faith comes from hearing the message, and the message is heard through the word of Christ" (Romans 10:14,17). It is through the proclamation of the "word of Christ," the gospel, found in Word and sacrament, that God has promised to work and strengthen faith. To wait for some other influence of God apart from those means is to wait for something God has not promised. "God was pleased through the foolishness of what was preached to save those who believe" (1 Corinthians 1:21).

Q: Since the word *sacrament* is not found in the Scriptures, why do we still use it?

A: It is true that the word *sacrament* is not a biblical term. It is a term that developed within the visible church through the centuries to describe the special blessings Jesus has given to his church. The word is used to describe special ceremonies that have visible elements connected to God's Word that give to us and seal our forgiveness of sins, life, and salvation. We would be perfectly free to abandon that term and develop another one if a better one could be found. However, that would create confusion and an apparent denial of what the church has taught about the sacraments. Although the word is not biblical, the teaching with which *sacrament* is connected is biblical.

2. We believe that through the gospel, the good news of Christ's atoning sacrifice for sinners, the Holy Spirit works faith in people, whose hearts are by nature hostile to God (1 Peter 1:23). Scripture teaches that "faith comes from hearing the message, and the message is heard through the word of Christ" (Romans 10:17). This Spirit-worked faith brings about a renewal in sinners and makes them heirs of eternal life in heaven.

Q: If hearing the gospel is the way the Holy Spirit works faith in people, how come so many hear the gospel and still do not believe?

A: The power of the Holy Spirit is always at work whenever the gospel is heard. That is why the author to the Hebrews could proclaim, "The word of God is living and active. Sharper than any double-edged sword, it penetrates even to dividing soul and spirit, joints and marrow" (Hebrews 4:12). Yet human nature possesses the power to reject that message. Jesus mourned over the many in Jerusalem who had resisted the power of the gospel. Overlooking Jerusalem, he said, "O Jerusalem, Jerusalem, you who kill the prophets and stone those sent to you, how often I have longed to gather your children together, as a hen gathers her chicks under her wings, but you were not willing" (Matthew 23:37). The Holy Spirit does not bring people to faith by an act of omnipotence that is irresistible but rather seeks to win and change human hearts by drawing those hearts to himself. Sadly, stubborn human nature resists this calling of the Holy Spirit.

Q: What is the "renewal in sinners" mentioned in this section?

A: When Adam and Eve fell into sin, they died spiritually. By their sin they changed from being friends of God to being enemies of God. Before their sin they were completely in harmony with God's will, but after their sin they were completely hostile to him and his will. This flaw became a part of their nature, and they were incapable of changing it. Their flawed nature was passed down to their children and then to each of us. The Scriptures tell us that "flesh gives birth to flesh" (John 3:6). But when we are brought to faith, a new self is born within us that is "created to be like God in true righteousness and holiness" (Ephesians 4:24). Adam and Eve renewed their relationship with God and became his friends when they trusted the promise of a Savior to come (Genesis 3:15). Every sinner renews that relationship when he or she believes in the Savior who has come, Jesus Christ. Even though we still struggle with the remnant of our sinful nature, and will until we are in heaven, that creation of a believing new self within each of us is the "renewal in sinners" referred to in this section.

 What does Scripture mean when it calls us heirs of heaven?

A: When the Holy Spirit brings us to faith in Jesus, we not only possess the acquittal of God, that is, not only are we justified, but at that moment we also "become heirs having the hope of eternal life" (Titus 3:7). As in earthly relationships, the heir is the one who will inherit the family estate. So too as children of God through Jesus, we stand to inherit the family estate of God, which is heaven with all its glory and joy. We will live there in the presence of our Father forever. Now we live as heirs entitled to that inheritance because of Jesus.

Q: If it is so important for people to hear the gospel, why does God allow so many to live their lives without ever hearing the message about Jesus?

A: We often blame God for the sinful activities of man. The history of this world reveals the repeated attempts of God to give away the truth of his gospel, but humans continue to turn away from it. As many as four times in human history the gospel may have been heard by people all over the world.

The first time would have been in the Garden of Eden when God announced the gospel for the first time after the first sin. Adam and Eve knew the gospel and shared it with their children. At the very beginning of human history, everyone knew the gospel!

Over time the vast majority of humankind turned from God's message of grace and forgiveness. God took action again to restore the knowledge of the gospel. The second time in human history that all the people of the world knew the gospel was after the flood. God had reduced the human population to eight souls. All of them witnessed God's great power and knew the truth and God's promise of the woman's seed to crush Satan's head.

But the pattern persisted. Humans once again chose to turn away from God and his promises. When once again the vast majority of the world lived in self-inflicted darkness, God spread the gospel a third time across the world through the work of the apostles. The apostles clearly took very seriously Jesus' command to preach the gospel to the entire world. Even a quick reading of the book of Acts will show the amazing distances and many peoples covered by just one apostle, the great missionary Paul. The events of Acts took place in a remarkably short amount of time—less than 50 years. The book of Acts records the efforts of Paul and his missionary team, but it is not an exhaustive travelogue of all the apostles. The rest of the apostles, as well as many other early Christians, also responded to Jesus' urgent appeal to reach out with the gospel. Some Christian traditions suggest that Christians went into Africa, India, China, and the British Isles.

Again, however, many places that once had the gospel lost it. Our own age is the fourth time in human history when the gospel stretches around the world. Technology and advances in mass communication help us in beaming the gospel around the globe. Clearly there are some barriers, such as language and culture, but it is amazing how far the gospel can reach in our electronic and technological world.

The story of this world's history clearly bears record to God's eager desire for the salvation of sinners around the globe. As Christians, we are part of God's plan. He uses us to share the gospel with others in many ways. But we must also confess how often we miss opportunities to share the gospel. God never fails to supply enough strength and resources to meet those opportunities. If the Christians of the United States would take seriously Jesus' command to spread the gospel to the world, everyone in the world would hear the gospel in a very short period of time.

3. We believe that also through the Sacrament of Baptism the Holy Spirit applies the gospel to sinners, giving them new life (Titus 3:5) and cleansing them from all sin (Acts 2:38). The Lord points to the blessing of Baptism when he promises, "Whoever believes and is baptized will be saved" (Mark 16:16). We believe that the blessing of Baptism is meant for all people (Matthew 28:19), including infants. Infants are born sinful (John 3:6) and therefore need to be born again, that is, to be brought to faith, through Baptism (John 3:5).

Q: **How is the water of Baptism able to give us new life and the forgiveness of sins?**

A: The water in itself is nothing special; it is simply a common and necessary part of our lives. But because the water is connected to God's Word, bears the promise of Jesus, and comes with the presence and power of the Holy Spirit, it is a wonderful water of life. God's Word makes it "the washing of rebirth and renewal by the Holy Spirit" (Titus 3:5). Because the water of Baptism bears the promise of Jesus, that water of Baptism "now saves you also" (1 Peter 3:21). As Peter promised on Pentecost, those who receive Baptism "receive the gift of the Holy Spirit" (Acts 2:38). When used as Christ commanded, the water of Baptism can do these things because it is a God-appointed means to connect the sinner to the cross of the Savior.

Q: Since most baptisms mentioned in Scripture were for adults, doesn't that speak against infant baptism?

A: It shouldn't surprise us that adult baptisms are mentioned more prominently in the New Testament, since what is recorded for us was the beginning of mission work as the message of Christ was reaching new places and lands. Unlike today, when most who are baptized are born into Christian families, during that first century of the Christian church the vast majority of adults were new converts to the faith.

At the same time, it is important to note that three times in Scripture baptisms include entire households (Acts 10, 16, and 1 Corinthians 1). The Greek word used to describe those households is a word that is never used in a situation where children are excluded. In fact, the typical household of that day would often include not only parents and children but also other relatives living with that family, as well as slaves and their families.

But most important, Jesus uses inclusive words when he institutes Baptism. He commands his disciples then and now to make disciples of "all nations" by baptizing and teaching (Matthew 28:19). On the first Pentecost, Peter copied the way his Lord spoke as he spoke of Baptism and its blessings: "The promise is for you and your children and for all who are far off—for all whom the Lord our God will call" (Acts 2:39).

Q: Since Jesus mentioned faith first and then Baptism in Mark 16:16, how can Baptism come before faith when we baptize infants?

A: Nowhere in Jesus' words in Mark 16 does he declare that he is stating an absolute rule of the order in which things must always take place. In Matthew 28:19,20, when Jesus institutes Baptism, he places baptizing before teaching. But that does not mean that he was setting up a rule that Baptism must always precede teaching. In both cases Jesus was simply mentioning how he expects his followers to carry out the work of sharing the gospel.

In addition, Scripture clearly indicates in John 3 and Titus 3 that Baptism has the power of working a second birth. The Bible uses that expression as another way of speaking about being brought from unbelief to faith. While faith may indeed precede Baptism for adults, with infants Baptism itself works faith through the power of the Spirit working through the gospel.

Q: If Baptism is a sacred act instituted by Christ, why didn't Christ baptize anyone during his ministry?

A: Remember that Jesus carried out his ministry among "the lost sheep of Israel" (Matthew 15:24). Many of them had been prepared for Jesus' ministry by the baptism of John the Baptist. Jesus did not set up a rival baptism. Instead, his ministry complemented the ministry of John. God established John's ministry to prepare for the coming of Jesus.

Only after Jesus' suffering, death, and resurrection did he institute Baptism. When the gospel was about to go out into the world of both Jews and Gentiles, Jesus instituted Baptism as one of the powerful tools of his church's work.

Q: Is there any way for someone to be saved who is not baptized?

A: What saves is faith in Jesus Christ. Baptism saves (1 Peter 3:21) not because it is a different way of salvation than through faith in Jesus but because it is one way such faith in Jesus can be created in the human heart. Scripture clearly tells us that through the washing of Baptism "the Spirit gives birth to spirit" (John 3:6). The Scripture also says that faith can be created by hearing the message of the gospel as it is preached and taught. Where faith has been created before Baptism, Baptism then becomes a wonderful personal gift that strengthens the faith that already exists. Therefore, if someone who has been brought to faith through the proclamation of the gospel dies before he or she learns of Baptism or has opportunity to be baptized, that person is still prepared to stand before God's judgment seat through faith in the Savior. The thief on the cross appears to be a prime example of someone brought to faith by the spoken Word who may not have had an opportunity to be baptized.

Q: Since Romans 10:17 tells us that "faith comes from hearing the message" of Christ, doesn't that rule out faith coming from Baptism?

A: Paul tells us in Galatians 3:26,27, "You are all sons of God through faith in Christ Jesus, for all of you who were baptized into Christ have clothed yourselves with Christ." When the gospel is spoken or preached, it works faith. It is the same as the gospel that comes to us with the Word and water in Baptism. The only difference in Baptism is that the gospel is accompanied by the visible sign of an earthly element. The message of Christ is the same, and the Holy Spirit works through it in the same way.

Since Paul doesn't specifically mention Baptism in Titus 3:5, how are we justified in saying that he is speaking about Baptism?

 The Greek word that is translated "washing" in Titus 3:5 is a synonym for the Greek word more commonly used for "Baptism" in the New Testament. The close similarity in wording and expression between Jesus' words in John 3:5,6 and Paul's words in Titus 3:5 is also another powerful indication that Baptism is being spoken of here.

If we teach that every child who is baptized automatically receives faith, aren't we then teaching irresistible grace?

It would be going beyond Scripture to say categorically that every child who has ever been baptized has always been brought to faith. That would be teaching irresistible grace. When we bring our children to the baptismal font, we are confident that the Holy Spirit works in the water and the Word to create faith and to plant the new self that trusts in Jesus as Savior. That such power of the Spirit is present in the water and Word of Baptism is clear from John 3 and Titus 3. God has not equipped us with any way to read the hearts of children or adults to determine whether saving faith exists or has been rejected. To quote Martin Luther in the Large Catechism, "We carry the child to the font with the purpose and the hope that he may believe, and we pray that God would give him faith." Our confidence is not that we can see into one heart and so determine what has happened in every case. Rather, we put our hope in the power of the Holy Spirit's working through the gospel.

Q: What should we do if someone refuses to have an infant baptized when we know how important Baptism is for that child?

A: Because we know the wonderful blessings God offers and gives in Baptism, we might at first think that the best course of action might be to take matters into our own hands and secretly baptize that infant ourselves. But we have a much better course of action. God has entrusted that child's physical and spiritual welfare to the parents and, in particular, the father, whom God desires to be the loving spiritual leader of his home: "Fathers, do not exasperate your children; instead, bring them up in the training and instruction of the Lord" (Ephesians 6:4). The most open and honest path is to continue to encourage those parents to consider their spiritual responsibilities toward their child. As Christians, we keep that family in our prayers at the same time. Showing those parents the beautiful gifts of Baptism as revealed in Scripture may be the best way to help them appreciate Baptism's blessings for their child.

Q: Who does Scripture say can administer Baptism?

A: The power of Baptism is in the promises of God, not in the human hand that administers it. Just as Christ has commanded every Christian to share the gospel, so the tools by which the gospel is shared have also been entrusted to every Christian.

Nevertheless, just because any Christian can administer Baptism, we should not abolish the practice of having our called public ministers perform all baptisms except those in cases of emergency. There are two sound biblical reasons for this practice. First, since "God is not a God of disorder but of peace" (1 Corinthians 14:33), God would have Baptism done "in a fitting and orderly way" (1 Corinthians 14:40). We have entrusted the public administration of the sacraments to our public ministers so that there is a careful system in place for the administering, recording, and witnessing of all baptisms. We don't want to create doubt in anyone's mind about whether he or she has been baptized at all or baptized properly.

Second, since the work of proclaiming the gospel has been entrusted to every believer (1 Peter 2:9), one believer should not function on behalf of another without a call to do so. As members of the universal priesthood of all believers, we call our pastors to publicly preach the gospel and administer the sacraments in Christ's name on our behalf. Such orderly public proclamation of the gospel was one of the reasons that Jesus instituted the public ministry.

Q: Is Baptism valid if it is administered in a church that teaches false doctrines?

A: The power in Baptism is the power of the Spirit who works through the Word connected to the water. The power is not dependent on those who use Baptism. We accept as valid all baptisms performed by churches that teach the Trinity. Clearly a confession of the Trinity is intimately connected to the application of Baptism. Even churches that teach falsely about the blessings of Baptism have a valid Baptism since the power is not dependent on our understanding but on God's promise. The false doctrines of such churches may hinder their members from enjoying all that Baptism has actually given them, but the baptisms are still valid.

The only exception to this would be if a church denied the doctrine of the Trinity so that "Father, Son, and Holy Spirit" were taught to be something other than what they plainly mean in Scripture. The power of the Word is not in the sounds of its syllables. If it were, Bible translations could not share the gospel with us, and we would have to be baptized using Greek. The power of the Word is in its God-established meaning. Any church that denies the doctrine of the Trinity may use the proper sounds and syllables, but it has emptied the Word of its meaning and so has destroyed the validity of its baptism. To call such baptisms valid in the face of such distortion of the meaning of the Word is to treat the syllables of God's Word as some magical incantation that works apart from its meaning. To put it another way: that church is no longer connecting the Word of God to the element. All it has is water!

4. We believe that all who join in the Sacrament of the Lord's Supper receive the true body and blood of Christ in, with, and under the bread and wine (1 Corinthians 10:16). This is true because, when the Lord instituted this sacrament, he said, "This is my body. This is my blood of the covenant, which is poured out for many for the forgiveness of sins" (Matthew 26:26,28). We believe that Christ's words of institution cause the real presence—not any human action. As believers receive his body and blood, they also receive the forgiveness of sins (Matthew 26:28) and the comfort and assurance that they are truly his own. Unbelievers also receive Christ's body and blood, but to their judgment (1 Corinthians 11:29).

Q: **What are we trying to say by the phrase "in, with, and under"?**

A: "In, with, and under" does not fix an exact spot where we can look and find the body and blood of Jesus somehow mingled with the bread and the wine. With this phrase we confess our belief that when Jesus said "This is my body" and "This is my blood," he truly meant what he said. Without trying to say how it can be, we confess that as we eat the bread and drink from the cup, we receive Christ's true body and blood once given and shed for us on the cross. At the same time, "in, with, and under" also protects us from the error of saying that the bread and wine magically disappear (transubstantiation) rather than remain together with the body and blood of our Lord.

Q: At what moment does Jesus' body and blood begin to be present in the observance of the Lord's Supper?

A: Jesus has not revealed to us the exact moment when the real presence of his body and blood begins. All that we can know for sure is that when we consecrate the bread and wine for this special Supper, distribute them, and eat and drink of them, we know that we have received his true body and blood. It is not necessary to know at what moment the sacramental union begins.

Q: Some substitute grape juice for wine in the Lord's Supper. Is that wrong?

A: There is no doubt that Jesus used wine at the first Lord's Supper. The custom of the Jews at the Passover meal was to use wine mixed with water. This is also clear from the time of the year in which the Passover took place. Grape harvest is in the autumn of the year, but the Passover is celebrated in the spring. In Jesus' day, the only way to preserve the "fruit of the vine" was to allow it to ferment into wine. The use of wine is also clear from 1 Corinthians 11. Some in the church in

Corinth were abusing the wine of the Lord's Supper and were getting drunk (1 Corinthians 11:21). Scripture does not forbid the use of alcoholic beverages, just their abuse. Therefore, to say that the use of wine is wrong would be clearly saying something the Scriptures do not say.

Yet, at the same time, nowhere in the accounts of the Lord's Supper does Scripture use the common Greek term for "wine." Rather, the Bible speaks of the "cup" or the "fruit of the vine." While it is clear that Jesus used fermented "fruit of the vine" at the first Lord's Supper, we would be in danger of legalistically going beyond Scripture to insist that unfermented "fruit of the vine" would render the sacrament invalid. Especially for the sake of those who struggle with alcoholism or who cannot take alcohol for another reason, this may be a legitimate option.

Perhaps even a better alternative for those who cannot drink alcohol is to make use of nonalcoholic wine, which has the added advantage of being fermented "fruit of the vine." The concern is always to raise as little doubt as possible about the Sacrament. We desire those who commune to concentrate on the miraculous gift they are receiving and not on what form of the earthly element is in the cup.

Q: **What is wrong with saying that the bread and the wine merely represent Christ's body and blood?**

A: To say that the bread and wine merely represent Christ's body and blood fails to take Jesus at his Word in the Supper. Jesus does not give any indication in the account from the upper room on that first Maundy Thursday that he is speaking figuratively as he distributes the bread and the cup. He speaks plainly and simply as he says, "This is my body" and "This is my blood." While it is true that what he says is astounding and that it goes beyond our human reason and understanding, we are always safe when we just take Jesus at his Word and promise.

In 1 Corinthians 10 and 11, the apostle Paul also helps us to see that we are not mistaken as we believe that Jesus is speaking plainly and not figuratively. In 1 Corinthians 10:16 Paul writes, "Is not the cup of thanksgiving for which we give thanks a participation in the blood of Christ? And is not the bread that we break a participation in the body of Christ?" Notice that Paul tells us there are two "participations" going on in the Lord's Supper. First, what is in the cup participates with the blood of Christ. Second, the bread participates with the body of Christ. There can be no real participation unless the body and blood of Christ are truly present in the cup and with the bread.

In 1 Corinthians 11:27 Paul warns, "Therefore, whoever eats the bread or drinks the cup of the Lord in an unworthy manner will be guilty of sinning against the body and blood of the Lord." If we come to the Supper with unbelieving or unrepentant hearts, we are not just sinning against the bread and wine, which merely represent Jesus' body and blood. We are "sinning against the body and blood of the Lord," which are truly present in this Supper.

Finally, Jesus describes the Lord's Supper as "the new covenant in my blood" (Luke 22:20). We do not have the option to change the details of any covenant or contract. This was the last will and testament of Jesus before his death. We are bound to take Jesus at his Word, even if we do not fully comprehend how the miracle of the Sacrament can be.

Those who reject the real presence usually do so not on the basis of the words of Scripture but on the basis of their human reason, which cannot comprehend how Jesus can mean what he clearly does say.

Q: Do we eat and drink Christ's body and blood in the Lord's Supper the same way that we eat and drink the bread and wine?

A: We receive his true body and blood as we eat and drink with our mouths. The bread and the wine are present in a very natural way, as any other food would be present in any meal. Jesus' body and blood, however, are present in a miraculous way according to the promise of Jesus. While we receive all four things with our mouths as we commune, nowhere does Scripture tell us to believe that we are tearing the body of Christ with our teeth or digesting his body and blood as we would any other earthly food. Those who say such things are often trying to ridicule the biblical teaching of the real presence.

Q: How can I receive forgiveness in the Lord's Supper if I already have received forgiveness in my baptism?

A: The gospel in the spoken or preached Word and in the Word that accompanies Baptism and the Lord's Supper is indeed the same gospel every time. Whenever the gospel is proclaimed to us, it gives us the gifts of forgiveness of sins, life, and salvation. God knows that since we continue to struggle with sin until we leave this life, he cannot communicate to us too often the gift of his forgiveness. In the announcement of our forgiveness, God helps us grow in faith and confidence, comforts us in times of difficulty, and assures us that we are forgiven. God is so rich in mercy that he does not want our doubts and sins to destroy our faith but comes to us again and again with his gifts of grace. This constant repetition of his gifts of grace is a reminder that we have a Savior about whom it is said, "A bruised reed he will not break, and a smoldering wick he will not snuff out" (Isaiah 42:3).

Q: Does the Lord's Supper actually give forgiveness to me or is it just an assurance and reminder of forgiveness?

A: Because the Lord's Supper is truly a means of grace in which the Holy Spirit is working through the gospel, it not only assures us of forgiveness but actually communicates to us the gift of forgiveness first won for us on the cross. The gospel in Word and sacrament is God's means to communicate from the cross to our hearts the actual gifts Christ has won for us. That is why Jesus proclaims to us as he distributes the cup, "This is my blood of the covenant, which is poured out for many for the forgiveness of sins" (Matthew 26:28).

Q: **If Jesus is ruling on a throne in heaven, how can he give me his body and blood in the Lord's Supper?**

A: Asking this question reveals a misunderstanding that unnecessarily confuses the issue. While Jesus does rule all things from the right hand of God, we must remember that the right hand of God is not some exalted chair placed in one certain spot in the universe. Consider the last words of the gospel of Matthew. There Jesus promised us, "And surely I am with you always, to the very end of the age" (Matthew 28:20). The *I* who was with the first disciples and who is still with us is the same *I* who visibly walked the earth for 33 years. The one who is with us always is the God-man Savior whom we know as Jesus. Just as God the Father and God the Holy Spirit are present everywhere and not just in the visible glory of heaven, so our Lord Jesus Christ, just as he promises, is present with us everywhere. His human nature is inseparably united to his divine nature ever since his incarnation within the body of Mary. The human nature of Jesus possesses all the attributes of his divine nature. That is why we can say that his rule at the right hand is not a rule in one place in heaven but is his position of power and authority. He exercises this power and authority now and is present everywhere as both our God and our brother.

While Jesus is omnipresent both as God and man and not stuck in some chair in heaven, that still does not explain the presence of his body and blood in the Lord's Supper. The unique presence of his body and blood with the bread and wine in his special Supper is true only because he promises it is. As the God-man Savior, he can do whatever he chooses to do. Therefore, he is more than able to keep his promise to be present in this special way as we receive his special Supper.

 How can unbelievers receive Jesus' body and blood in Holy Communion since they don't believe Jesus' promise that his body and blood are truly present?

A: Enjoying the blessings of the sacraments does depend on our faith. Without faith in what is being offered in either Baptism or the Lord's Supper, there is no benefit for the one who receives those sacraments.

However, there is a difference between enjoying the blessings of the sacraments and the reality (or validity) of the sacraments. God's gifts and promises are true even if no one believes them. "What if some did not have faith? Will their lack of faith nullify God's faithfulness? Not at all! Let God be true, and every man a liar" (Romans 3:3,4). The body and blood that our Lord Jesus promises to be present in the Sacrament will be present even if all those who come refuse to believe his faithfulness. That is why Paul warns that someone who comes to the Lord's Table in an unworthy manner, that is, in unbelief or impenitence, still receives the Lord's body and blood. But by not recognizing what he or she is receiving, he or she "eats and drinks judgment on himself" (1 Corinthians 11:29).

 Where in Scripture does God determine the proper age for children to begin receiving the Lord's Supper?

A: Nowhere does Scripture set an absolute age requirement for children before they can begin to receive the Lord's Supper. What we know from Scripture is that a person who approaches the Lord's Table needs to be able "to examine himself before he eats of the bread and drinks of the cup" (1 Corinthians 11:28). This speaks of having attained a certain amount of spiritual maturity through instruction in the Word. Any communicant should be able to carry out such spiritual self-examination. Yet Scripture does not give us a specific age at which such maturity will be present.

Q: Whom does Scripture say can consecrate and distribute Holy Communion?

A: Just as it is with Baptism, the validity of the Lord's Supper does not depend on the person who consecrates and distributes it but rather on the promise and the power of Jesus.

Just as with Baptism, there is good reason why we typically entrust the administration of the Lord's Supper to our called pastors. The same two sound biblical reasons exist for this practice. First, since "God is not a God of disorder but of peace" (1 Corinthians 14:33), God would have this important Sacrament done "in a fitting and orderly way" (1 Corinthians 14:40). One reason we have entrusted the public administration of the sacraments to our public ministers is so that there is a careful and orderly way for this precious sacrament to be distributed to God's people.

Second, since the work of proclaiming the gospel has been entrusted to every believer (1 Peter 2:9), no one believer should function on behalf of another without a call to do so. As members of the universal priesthood of all believers, we call our pastors to publicly preach the gospel and administer the sacraments in Christ's name on our behalf. Such orderly public proclamation of the gospel was one of the reasons that Jesus instituted the public ministry.

5. We believe that the Lord gave his Word and the sacraments of Baptism and the Lord's Supper for a purpose. He commanded his followers, "Go and make disciples of all nations, baptizing them in the name of the Father and of the Son and of the Holy Spirit, and teaching them to obey everything I have commanded you" (Matthew 28:19,20). Through God's Word and sacraments he preserves and extends the holy Christian church throughout the world. Believers should therefore be diligent and faithful in the use of these divinely established means of grace for themselves and in their mission outreach to others. These are the only means through which immortal souls are brought to faith and to life in heaven.

Q: Since we practice close communion (also called closed communion), won't we drive people away and frustrate the mission purpose of one of the sacraments?

A: For many centuries, Christians have recognized that there is a difference between Baptism and the Lord's Supper in just this area. Baptism has long been called the sacrament of initiation; it is the sacrament by which souls are brought into the kingdom. The Lord's Supper has been called the sacrament of confirmation; it is the sacrament by which those already within the kingdom are strengthened.

Those distinctions have their biblical origins in the different way each sacrament was instituted. Baptism was instituted with an encouragement to go to all nations and baptize them in order to make disciples from those nations. However, the Lord's Supper was instituted in a close circle of disciples who had been trained and taught by the Lord for a considerable amount of time. Very much like the ancient Passover meal at which it was instituted, the Lord's Supper is a meal for those who are already united as family within the flock of Christ.

That is the very point Paul drives home in 1 Corinthians 10:17: "Because there is one loaf, we, who are many, are one body, for we all partake of the one loaf." The Lord's Supper not only strengthens our unity in faith with one another as it draws us to Christ, but at the same time, it publicly confesses that unity of faith. When we approach the Lord's Table, we not only commune with Christ but make a public confession that we share a common faith with those communing with us before that altar. There is both a vertical—with Christ—and a horizontal—with one another—fellowship taking place whenever we commune. That is why we ask those who wish to receive the Lord's Supper with us first to learn what we believe and teach. Then they are ready to join us in making their confession of the same teachings when they receive the Lord's Supper with us. That is one of the reasons why even those who grow up in our churches are first instructed before they commune.

Of course, there is even another concern behind this scriptural practice of close communion. We must also be concerned that those who commune are aware of the real presence of Christ's body and blood in the Supper. Those who receive the Lord's Supper without recognizing the body and blood of the Lord bring on themselves judgment instead of blessing (1 Corinthians 11:29).

It is true that our biblical practice of close communion causes many to disagree with us. Often those who do not understand this biblical practice become angry with us and perhaps no longer worship with us. But we believe that we must be faithful to the Scriptures and to the Lord's institution no matter what others may think.

Q: Do public ministers or members of the congregation have the chief responsibility in using the means of grace to reach out to others?

A: While our public ministers are called to be overseers for our souls as they care for us with the means of grace (Hebrews 13:17), they are also called to use those means of grace to equip each believer for service to Christ and his gospel (Ephesians 4:11-13).

Ever since the water of Baptism ushered us into Christ's kingdom, every Christian is a royal priest of God. As such, we have all been called to "declare the praises of him who called [us] out of darkness into his wonderful light" (1 Peter 2:9). Therefore, the ministry of the gospel—the use of the means of grace—is the privilege and responsibility of every Christian. That is true both when we use that gospel to encourage those already within the kingdom as well as when we seek the other sheep Christ has not yet gathered into his flock (John 10:16).

Instead of wondering who has the "chief responsibility," it is much better for us, as Christians, to be living with our eyes and ears open so that we can "make the most of every opportunity" (Colossians 4:5) that God gives us.

Q: Won't God save others without the means of grace by using some other method?

A: God has not revealed that he plans to save anyone apart from the means of grace. "God was pleased through the foolishness of what was preached to save those who believe" (1 Corinthians 1:21). He has not revealed that he plans to use anyone to share that message other than those whom he has already brought to faith. "How can they hear without someone preaching to them?" (Romans 10:14). Except for a few angelic exceptions at Christmas and Easter, the privilege to share the message of the gospel is ours. Wouldn't it be fool-ish arrogance on our part to sit back and expect God to reach those who are still lost in another way than through the gospel shared by those who already confess Jesus' name? We are heirs of God's grace. God has given us work to do, which angels themselves oversee with rejoicing (Luke 15:10). Our witnesses can make an eternal difference in the lives of oth-ers. God encourages that. Though the world may reject us for what we share, by God's free grace those who lead others to righteousness will shine "like the stars for ever and ever" (Daniel 12:3).

6. We reject any views that look for the revelation of the grace of God and salvation apart from the gospel as found in the Scriptures. We reject any views that look for the Holy Spirit to work faith apart from the means of grace. We likewise reject the view that the law is a means of grace.

Q: Where does Scripture indicate that God will work only through the means of grace?

A: In addition to what was stated in the answer to the preceding question, we can find God's plan in the story of the rich man and Lazarus (Luke 16:19ff). The rich man was sent to hell. While he was there, he suggested that God made a mistake by not bringing him to faith by some special signs and wonders. He then requested that his living brothers be given such a miraculous call to faith. But Abraham spoke for God and answered the rich man: "They have Moses and the Prophets; let them listen to them" (verse 29). God has appointed his means of grace by which we will come to faith. A sinner ignores such means only to his or her eternal judgment.

 Since the Holy Spirit is God and can do anything, why do we limit him by saying that he won't work faith apart from the means of grace?

A: The question here is not what God can do. The obvious answer to that is that he can do "whatever pleases him" (Psalm 115:3), since "nothing is impossible with God" (Luke 1:37). The question here is what God has told us and has promised us he will do. Please read the previous two questions and answers. Remember what Paul tells us in Romans 10:17: "Faith comes from hearing the message, and the message is heard through the word of Christ." God himself is not bound, but we are bound to use the means of grace because God has not promised that he will work on human hearts in any other way.

Q: Why isn't the law also a means of grace since it too is divinely revealed?

A: By "means of grace" we mean those tools that God uses to create or strengthen faith. While the Holy Spirit clearly uses the law to convict hearts of sin (John 16:8), that, in itself, does not work faith or strengthen faith. In 2 Corinthians 3:6, Paul labels the law "the letter" and tells us, "The letter kills, but the Spirit gives life." It is through the good news of the gospel found in Word and sacrament that the Spirit gives us life in Jesus. Although the law is divinely inspired and the Spirit is at work in it, when it comes to the work of creating and saving faith, only the gospel has that power. As Paul tells the Thessalonian Christians, "But we ought always to thank God for you, brothers loved by the Lord, because from the beginning God chose you to be saved through the sanctifying work of the Spirit and through belief in the truth. He called you to this through our gospel" (2 Thessalonians 2:13,14).

Q: How do some claim that the Holy Spirit works apart from the means of grace?

A: Some believe that the Spirit speaks to them more directly than through the means of grace. They expect to hear the Spirit speak to them through dreams, visions, or voices that they hear in their minds. While God has at times used such methods to communicate to his inspired apostles and prophets, there is no promise from God that he will speak to us through such direct means in order to bring people to faith or keep us in the faith. In fact, such occurrences were typically not to bring someone to faith or strengthen their faith. Such special revelations were given before and during the time of the writing of Scripture as God sought to communicate his will to those who did not have the complete revelation we now have in the Bible.

When God called the apostle Paul to faith in the miraculous way he did (Acts 9), God used the spoken external Word to communicate with Paul. The Lord pointed out through audible words that the message of the gospel Paul was persecuting was in fact a persecution of the Son of God himself. Then God sent Ananias to Paul, and Ananias baptized him.

Therefore, since God has not promised to work or strengthen faith through such direct means or has not even promised to any specific Christian that he or she will ever have any such dreams or visions, it is important for us to make use of the means he has promised to use: the gospel in Word and sacraments.

Those who claim to have special revelation from God must also search the Scriptures to see if their revelation contradicts the written Word of God. Anything that is contrary to the written Word is from Satan and cannot be trusted.

7. We reject the view that babies should not be baptized and that they cannot believe in Christ (Luke 18:15-17). We reject the view that baptism must be by immersion.

Q: Why do so many reject infant baptism?

A: There are several reasons why people reject infant baptism. One of the most common reasons is the failure to see Baptism as a means of grace that communicates Christ's saving love from his cross to our hearts. If Baptism is nothing more than a symbol to remind us of what Christ has done, then it is wasted on infants who cannot recognize or understand the symbol. But if Baptism is indeed the "washing of rebirth and renewal by the Holy Spirit" (Titus 3:5) that Paul tells us it is, then all ages can benefit from the powerful work of the sacrament of Baptism.

Another reason that many reject infant baptism is that they misunderstand original sin. They do not recognize that outward sinful actions are not what make us sinners. Such outward sinful actions are simply the evidence of the sinful state of our human hearts that already exists. Although children may not have had opportunity to fully show the sinfulness of their hearts yet, it doesn't mean that they are not already sinners. King David so clearly proclaimed the truth of the sinful state in which we enter this world: "Surely I was sinful at birth, sinful from the time my mother conceived me" (Psalm 51:5). It is because of that natural state of sinfulness that Paul could also write, "We were by nature objects of wrath" (Ephesians 2:3). Baptism is God's wonderful application of his grace that frees us from being objects of wrath and makes us instead objects of his mercy which are brought into the kingdom of his grace.

A third reason many reject infant baptism is that they do not understand the biblical definition of faith. They believe that faith is the conscious decision of the human will after God has presented the message of his gospel. Obviously, if faith is a conscious decision of human will, then infants could not believe and Baptism could not work faith in them. However, Scripture clearly proclaims that faith is a "gift of God" (Ephesians 2:8) that is worked by the Holy Spirit. We do not choose God, but he chooses us and brings us to faith (1 Corinthians 1:26ff). Since faith is a miracle worked by the power of the Holy Spirit as the gospel is proclaimed, then such a miracle can be performed not only in adult hearts but also in the hearts of infants.

Q: How does Luke 18:15-17 teach that infants can believe?

A: Luke mentions that many of those brought to Jesus were "babies." The Greek word he uses is the word for "very young children," in fact, it is often used even for "the unborn in the mother's womb." Then notice what Jesus says next about these little "babies" who were brought to him. He mentions that "the kingdom of God belongs to such as these" (18:16). The kingdom of heaven belongs to no one, except through faith. By nature we are objects of God's wrath (Ephesians 2:3), not citizens of his kingdom. Only through faith in Jesus Christ do we become children of God within God's saving kingdom

(Galatians 3:26). If the "kingdom of God belongs to such as these," then little ones—such as those "babies"—must be able to be brought to faith in their Savior.

Q: **What is immersion?**

A: Immersion is the method of applying the water in Baptism by which the person is entirely submerged beneath the water.

Q: **Why is it wrong to insist on immersion when immersion may have been a common practice in the early church?**

A: Yes, immersion was an ancient method for applying the water in Baptism, but throughout the history of the church, it has never been the only way that baptisms have been performed. Most important, not even once in all of Scripture is a particular method of applying the water mentioned. Even when the Bible speaks of the one baptizing and the one being baptized going down into the water and coming up out of it (for example, Acts 8:38,39), it tells us nothing about how the water was applied during the baptism itself.

The Greek word used most commonly for "baptism" or "to baptize" did have as its original meaning "to put something completely under water," but by the time of the writing of the New Testament, that word had taken on a broader meaning of "putting water on something" without specifying in what way that had to be done. Therefore, to insist on a particular method of applying water in Baptism is to go beyond Scripture. Perhaps even worse, it introduces a law where the gospel should dominate.

8. We reject all teachings that the Sacrament of the Altar offers nothing more than signs and symbols of Jesus' sacrifice, thereby denying that Christ's true body and blood are received in the Lord's Supper. We reject the view that those who eat the body of Christ in the sacrament merely receive Christ spiritually by faith. We reject the claim that unbelievers and hypocrites do not receive the true body and blood of Jesus in the Sacrament.

Q: Since we are saved by faith, not by church rites, why must the Sacrament of the Altar be more than a sign or symbol?

A: We are saved through faith in Jesus alone, but we became believers because the Holy Spirit worked through the means of grace. The gospel in Word and sacrament is the means by which God takes the blessings of Christ at his cross, brings those gifts to our hearts, and thereby works or strengthens faith in us to trust those gifts.

To call the sacraments nothing but church rites is to forget that Baptism and the Lord's Supper are divinely instituted means for communicating to our hearts the grace of Jesus Christ. To speak of the Lord's Supper as a mere sign or symbol is to treat it as something far less than Scripture declares it to be. The Lord's Supper is and until the Last Day will always remain the "new covenant in [his] blood" (Luke 22:20) by which we receive all the blessings Jesus has won for us: forgiveness of sins, life, and salvation.

Q: What is wrong with saying that we receive Christ's body and blood merely spiritually in the Lord's Supper?

A: Those who say that we receive Christ's body and blood merely spiritually use such language to deny the real presence of Christ's body and blood in the Lord's Supper. Those who use such terminology teach that Christ's body and blood can only be found in heaven. They teach that when we go to the Lord's Supper, we must by faith ascend to heaven and in a "spiritual" way receive his body and blood since they are not actually present in the Sacrament.

Q: How can unbelievers and hypocrites receive the body and blood of Jesus since they don't believe the promise Jesus made when he gave us his Supper?

A: Unbelievers and hypocrites forfeit the blessings that Jesus' body and blood bring in his Supper, but by their lack of faith, they do not cancel what the Supper is. "Therefore, whoever eats the bread or drinks the cup of the Lord in an unworthy manner will be guilty of sinning against the body and blood of the Lord" (1 Corinthians 11:27). Notice that Christ's body and blood are present whether someone believes it or not. Those communing in an unworthy manner will sin against the body and blood if they refuse to believe it. Christ's promise is what makes the Supper what it is, not our faith or lack of it.

9. We reject the doctrine of transubstantiation, which teaches that the substance of the bread and wine are changed entirely into the body and blood of Christ. Scripture teaches that all communicants receive both the bread and wine and the body and blood of Christ (1 Corinthians 10:16).

Q: How does 1 Corinthians 10:16 teach that we receive Christ's body and blood and bread and wine in Holy Communion?

A: First Corinthians 10:16 says, "The cup of thanksgiving for which we give thanks" is "a participation in the blood of Christ," and the passage tells us that "the bread that we break" is "a participation in the body of Christ." This verse is talking about the consecrated bread and wine distributed to those who are communing, and yet it still speaks of "the cup," that is, the wine in the cup, and "the bread" as still present. The passage also says that "the cup" and "the blood of Christ" and "the bread" and "the body of Christ" have a "participation" with one another. If the wine and bread have been completely changed into Christ's blood and body, then there is nothing left to *participate* with. A "participation" clearly demands at least two things to be present together. This passage clearly tells us that there are two "participations" going on in the Lord's Supper: the bread and the body of Christ and the wine and the blood of Christ. Therefore, every time we receive the Lord's Supper we are receiving those four things.

Q: What is wrong with the teaching of transubstantiation since it at least takes seriously the presence of Jesus' body and blood?

A: While it is true that transubstantiation takes very seriously the real presence of Christ's body and blood in the Sacrament, the problem is that it goes beyond the words of Scripture. Transubstantiation attempts to explain in an almost magical way how Christ's body and blood are present in the Supper. Nowhere does Scripture explain to us how Jesus fulfills his promise of being truly present with his body and blood in the Supper. Transubstantiation also denies the "participation" of the elements (see previous answer).

The teaching of transubstantiation leads to other problems as well. The Roman Catholic Church teaches that the priest in his ordination is given the special power to transform the bread and wine into Christ's body and blood as he says the proper words at the proper time in the celebration of the mass. The danger is that the attention of the one communing is taken off of Christ, whose promise is the real power of the Lord's Supper, and focused instead on some almost magical power supposedly entrusted to the priest. In addition, the mass then becomes a special sacrifice—additional to the one sacrifice of Christ on Calvary—for the sins of people. This makes atonement for sin dependent upon the action of a priest and minimizes Christ's one sacrifice for all sins (Hebrews 7:27 and 9:26-28).

Furthermore, because the Roman Catholic Church teaches that the priest changes the bread and wine into Christ's body and blood, the bread and wine remain body and blood even if there is no reception of the elements. This leads to worship of the consecrated elements, which the church believes, apart from eating and drinking, are the body and blood of Christ. This can be seen when the bread, or the host, is paraded in events such as a Corpus Christi celebration. Jesus never said, "This worship." He said, "Take eat" and "Take drink."

All these problems are evidence of the trouble we cause if we insist on going beyond what Scripture has told us.

10. We reject any attempt to set the precise moment within the celebration of the Lord's Supper when the body and blood of Christ become present. We therefore reject the view that one must believe that Christ's body and blood are present as soon as the words of consecration have been spoken and the view that one must believe that Christ's body and blood become present only at the moment of eating and drinking.

Q: Why isn't it important to know the pre-cise moment when Christ's body and blood are present in the Lord's Supper?

A: Other than satisfying our curiosity, we do not need to know the exact moment when the real presence begins. We need to know that when the Lord's Supper is celebrated and when we eat and drink of the bread and wine, in a miraculous way we also receive the very body and blood of Christ. Beyond that, the reminder of Psalm 131:1,2 is fitting to hear: "My heart is not proud, O LORD, my eyes are not haughty; I do not concern myself with great matters or things too wonderful for me. But I have stilled and quieted my soul; like a weaned child with its mother."

Q: What is the purpose of speaking the words of consecration over the bread and wine?

A: While the original promise of Christ, not our exact repeating of certain sounds or syllables, makes the Lord's Supper valid, it is good practice to speak the words of consecration for several reasons. First, the words of consecration set aside otherwise ordinary bread and wine for special use in the Supper. Second, repeating the words of consecration announces to all that we are celebrating the same Supper that our Lord instituted that first Maundy Thursday evening in that upper room with his first disciples. Third, with those words we confess clearly our conviction that, because of Jesus' promise, we will receive his very body and blood together with that bread and wine.

Q: What should we do with the bread and wine that is left over after the Lord's Supper?

A: Scripture does not lead us to conclude that Christ's body and blood continue to be in the elements apart from the consecration, distribution, and reception of the elements. After the celebration of the Sacrament, the bread and wine are once again bread and wine. Yet we should always deal reverently with the elements that were part of the celebration of the Lord's Supper. Just as those in the congregation who are entrusted with caring for the communionware treat those items with love, so should the bread and wine that is leftover be treated with care as well. The bread that remains is normally kept for the next time communion is celebrated. While the wine in the flagons, the pitchers used in the Lord's Supper, and in the unused individual cups can be saved for a future celebration of the Lord's Supper, the wine left over in the common cup is usually disposed of. Some follow the custom of pouring the contents of the cup out on the ground instead of pouring the contents down a regular drain. This custom shows respect for the wine that has been used for a very special purpose. But no matter what is done at that time, we are not wasting the blood of Christ or disposing of it since we are no longer celebrating the Lord's Supper.

Additional Reading for This Section:

Holy Spirit: The Giver of Life by John F. Vogt

Baptism: My Adoption into God's Family by Gaylin R. Schmeling

Baptized into God's Family: The Doctrine of Infant Baptism for Today by A. Andrew Das

The Lord's Supper by Martin Chemnitz (translated by J. A. O. Preus)

Section VII.
CHURCH AND MINISTRY

1. We believe that there is one holy Christian church, which is the temple of God (1 Corinthians 3:16) and the body of Christ (Ephesians 1:23; 4:12). The members of this one church are all those who are the "sons of God through faith in Christ Jesus" (Galatians 3:26). The church, then, consists only of believers, or saints, whom God accepts as holy for the sake of Jesus' righteousness, which has been credited to them (2 Corinthians 5:21). These saints are scattered throughout the world. All people who believe that Jesus is their Savior from sin are members of the holy Christian church, regardless of the nation, race, or church body to which they belong.

Q: What does it mean when Scripture labels the holy Christian church "the temple of God"?

A: When Scripture labels the holy Christian church "the temple of God," it presents a beautiful double picture. A "temple" is the special dwelling place of God. In a very special way, through his means of grace, Christ dwells with his people. He promises us in Matthew 18:20, "Where two or three come together in my name, there am I with them." But there is even more. Not only does Jesus dwell within his church when we gather in his name, but he also dwells in each believer. From the moment the Holy Spirit works faith in the heart of an individual, he or she personally also becomes a temple in which God lives. "Do you not know that your body is a temple of the Holy Spirit, who is in you, whom you have received from God?" (1 Corinthians 6:19). In this double way, each Christian individually and all believers together are "the temple of God"—the special dwelling place of God. While God is present everywhere in his omnipresence, in a special way he has promised his believers that he will be with them and within them to bless and protect them always. Labeling the holy Christian church "the temple of God" is one more beautiful assurance of our final and eternal victory through our Lord Jesus Christ.

Q: ■ **What does it mean when Scripture labels the** ■ **holy Christian church "the body of Christ"?**

A: Scripture teaches two beautiful truths when it labels the church "the body of Christ." First, calling believers the body of Christ vividly paints the comforting truth of the close connection between believers and Jesus. As closely and intimately as our physical heads are connected to our bodies, so close is the spiritual connection between the Savior and all who cling to him by faith. The loving care and protection of the body by Christ, its head, is a recurring theme of many of God's promises.

At the same time, calling believers the body of Christ not only stresses our close connection to Christ, our head, but also impresses on us the close connection between each believer. Believers are united into one spiritual body in Christ. The apostle Paul wrote, "The body is a unit, though it is made up of many parts; and though all its parts are many, they form one body. So it is with Christ. For we were all baptized by one Spirit into one body—whether Jews or Greeks, slave or free—and we were all given the one Spirit to drink"

(1 Corinthians 12:12,13). We are intimately joined with every other believer of all time and of all places in a close, invisible fellowship. With this metaphor, Scripture encourages us, as believers, to use our talents and spiritual gifts to serve one another and to build up the body of Christ.

Q: Why does it matter which church you belong to if members of the holy Christian church are found in every Christian denomination?

A: We thank God that wherever the gospel is taught, even though it may be surrounded by errors, God will see to it that his Word does not return empty. Despite the errors that are present, we trust that God will always save some.

But that does not change the danger of the mixture of truth and error. It is simply spiritual poison together with spiritual food. False teaching spreads "like gangrene" (2 Timothy 2:17). It is always at work to destroy the spiritual health of those who hear it or believe it. While we give thanks for the miracle of the Holy Spirit when he preserves the faith of some despite the very real danger of false doctrine, Scripture again and again warns believers of false teachers and errors. Such errors and those that teach them cost many their faith. That is why we follow the loving encouragement of the apostle Peter: "Like newborn babies, crave pure spiritual milk, so that by it you may grow up in your salvation, now that you have tasted that the Lord is good" (1 Peter 2:2,3). Just as we desire the healthiest food and drink for the temporal health of our bodies, so we desire healthy food and drink for our souls. God's desire is that we learn to love the taste of the pure milk of his gospel grace so greatly that we crave nothing for our souls but that pure spiritual milk.

Q: Aren't those who sincerely seek God and trust in the teachings of non-Christian religions also included in the church?

A: There is no doubt that in non-Christian religions there are many who are very sincerely seeking to find peace of conscience and a relationship with God. The devotion and discipline of their lives often put us to shame as Christians. Nevertheless, sincerely clinging to error cannot save anyone. Faith, even devout faith, saves only because of the object or idea to which it clings. All are born dead in sin with an inborn hostility towards the true God. There is and ever will be only one way to be saved. Jesus says that so clearly in John 14:6: "I am the way and the truth and the life. No one comes to the Father except through me." Only through the perfect life and innocent death of Jesus Christ has the path been opened to the only true God. Only when the Holy Spirit brings us to repentance for our sins and to trust in Jesus as our Savior can we claim to be children of God. Apart from faith in Jesus Christ, no salvation exists.

Q: Why would we exclude from the Christian church an unbeliever who is living a very moral life but just has not yet learned to know Jesus?

A: Humankind's basic idea of religion is that we somehow make up for our sins by doing more good than evil. However, apart from faith in Christ, "there is no one who does good, not even one" (Romans 3:12). Jesus tells us plainly in John 15:5, "I am the vine; you are the branches. If a man remains in me and I in him, he will bear much fruit; apart from me you can do nothing." Because we are by nature dead in sin (Ephesians 2:1) and hostile to God (Romans 8:7), even the best any human can produce is imperfect and flawed. Only Christ provides full forgiveness for human sin, flaws, and imperfections. Without faith in Jesus, even an apparently moral life is not enough. Listen to what the prophet Isaiah had to say about even his best works: "All of us have become like one who is unclean, and all our righteous acts are like filthy rags" (Isaiah 64:6). While living an outwardly moral life may seem to the unbeliever to be the sure path to God, the book of Proverbs has something to say about that which seems so right to human beings: "There is a way that seems right to a man, but in the end it leads to death" (14:12).

2. We believe that this holy Christian church is a reality, although it is not an external, visible organization. Because "man looks at the outward appearance, but the LORD looks at the heart" (1 Samuel 16:7), only the Lord knows "those who are his" (2 Timothy 2:19). The members of the holy Christian church are known only to God; we cannot distinguish between true believers and hypocrites. The holy Christian church is therefore invisible and cannot be identified with any one church body or with the total membership of all church bodies.

Q: Why can't we distinguish between hypocrites and true believers?

A: "Man looks at the outward appearance, but the LORD looks at the heart" (1 Samuel 16:7). If we could see the true inner thoughts and beliefs of other human beings, only then could we accurately identify who are believers and who are nothing but hypocrites. Without such knowledge, our attempts to separate the true believers from the hypocrites would be spiritually disastrous. A believer will confess Jesus as the Savior and live as a Christian, but a hypocrite will also confess Jesus and live as a Christian. We cannot look within the thoughts of either of them to be certain who is a believer and who is a hypocrite. When a person says he or she does not believe in Jesus and does not live as a Christian, we can judge that person to be unchristian. But we can make that judgment only on the basis of what a person does and says, not on the basis of what he or she thinks. That is why we will always want to accept everyone's confession of Christ as sincere unless he or she proves insincere by open and continued impenitence. "The Lord knows those who are his" (2 Timothy 2:19).

 Are we identifying the WELS with the holy Christian church since we claim to be a true visible church?

A: We are convinced that within our fellowship we do not compromise any doctrine of Scripture. That is what it means to be a true visible church. Yet it would be arrogant to identify one church body with the holy Christian church. That is confusing a visible church body with the *invisible* holy Christian church.

Wherever there are souls that cling alone to the righteousness won for them by the life, death, and resurrection of the eternal Son of God, there will be believers. Such believers will be found in all Christian churches, wherever the gospel of Christ is proclaimed and taught, even where doctrinal errors are present. Despite the deadly dangers that those false doctrines pose for Christians within such churches, we thank God that the Holy Spirit can still use what remains of the truth to preserve faith in some, if not many.

Every time in worship that we speak the Apostles' or Nicene Creed, we confess that we do believe in this holy Christian church that is made up of uncountable believers on earth as well as those already in heaven. We trust that those who hear the gospel within the WELS are numbered among those saints in Christ. At the same time, we thank God that many, many more who are not part of our church body are also numbered among those saints in Christ.

Q: Why can't we identify the holy Christian church with the total membership of all Christian church bodies?

A: To identify the holy Christian church with the total membership of all Christian church bodies would again be confusing the visible church with the invisible church. Sad to say, Satan plants hypocrites wherever Jesus plants his true believers. The parable of the weeds in Matthew 13:24ff teaches that clearly. It will be this way until judgment day, when the sheep or believers are gathered at Jesus' right and the goats or unbelievers are at his left (Matthew 25:31ff). In the final judgment, we will be able to tell who belonged to Jesus Christ and who did not. Many whose names were on the membership roles of Christian churches but who did not trust in Christ will find themselves forever on the outside of God's eternal kingdom. Despite having spent much time in the visible fellowship of the Christian church, many on the Last Day will hear these words from Jesus: "I tell you the truth, I don't know you" (Matthew 25:12). Only the power of the gospel can keep genuine faith and hope alive.

Q: What do we mean when we call the holy Christian church invisible?

A: We see people gather around the means of grace, and we trust that in all such Christian gatherings there are at least some true believers present. Yet only God can see faith in Christ within believers. Therefore, the real church remains invisible to our human eyes until the Last Day.

3. We believe that the presence of the holy Christian church nevertheless can be recognized. Wherever the gospel is preached and the sacraments are administered, the holy Christian church is present, for through the means of grace true faith is produced and preserved (Isaiah 55:10,11). The means of grace, therefore, are called the marks of the church.

Q: **If the holy Christian church is invisible, how can we say that we recognize its presence?**

A: Because of God's promise that his Word will not return empty (Isaiah 55:10,11), we trust that wherever people are gathered around the Word and sacrament, some believers will be present. While we cannot know who exactly the believers are, these "marks of the church"—the gospel in Word and sacrament—help us recognize where the church is present.

Q: **What do we mean when we label the means of grace "the marks of the church"?**

A: Believers will gather around the gospel in Word and sacrament. Wherever you find the gospel in Word and sacrament, there you will find true believers. In this way, the Word and sacrament are "the marks of the church." They are the "marks" we look for in order to know where Christ's church is present.

Q: **Since so many Christian church bodies confess teachings different from the Scriptures, are we saying that the Holy Spirit uses false doctrine to save sinners?**

A: The Holy Spirit does not use the errors in those churches to save sinners. In fact, every false doctrine is a bit of poison that threatens to rob a believer of his or her spiritual life. The more false doctrine that exists in a church, the greater the danger that such poison will destroy the faith of a believer. Nevertheless, because the truth of the gospel is still at times heard even in the midst of error, the power of that gospel can preserve faith in the hearts of some—and at times, many.

4. We believe that it is the Lord's will that Christians meet regularly to build one another up by using the means of grace together (Hebrews 10:24,25) and to work for the spread of the gospel into all the world (Mark 16:15). Since these visible gatherings (for example, congregations and synods) use the means of grace, they are called churches. They bear this name, however, only because of the true believers present in them (1 Corinthians 1:2).

Q: Why is it so important to gather together with fellow Christians?

A: Believers gain great spiritual benefit when they meditate on God's Word in the privacy of their own homes. The Holy Spirit works through such daily meditation on the saving Word of God. But God also desires believers to gather together with their fellow believers. God's Word is clear about that: "Let us not give up meeting together, as some are in the habit of doing, but let us encourage one another—and all the more as you see the Day approaching" (Hebrews 10:25).

What are the rich blessings of our "meeting together"? First, as believers come together with other fellow Christians, they gain from the experience and insight of others. One believer may have a greater insight than another in understanding Scripture or in applying it to daily life. Believers need one another. Paul speaks about this beautiful chain reaction within the body of Christ when he writes, "Praise be to the God and Father of our Lord Jesus Christ, the Father of compassion and the God of all comfort, who comforts us in all our troubles, so that we can comfort those in any trouble with the comfort we ourselves have received from God" (2 Corinthians 1:3,4). Believers share the comfort and power of the gospel with others even when they don't have the opportunity to speak to others personally. As they sing hymns together, confess their faith together, and speak prayers together, they give encouragement to one another in the race of faith. Even sitting in the pew on a particular Sunday morning is an encouragement that others share a common faith in Christ.

Second, the sacraments were intended to be used by groups of Christians rather than by one believer in the privacy of his or her home. The sacraments presume there to be at least two people present—one who administers the sacrament and one who receives its blessings. This is especially true of the Lord's Supper. Believers confess a unity of faith when they receive the Sacrament together (1 Corinthians 10:16,17).

We are, after all, parts of the body of Christ. A separated member of Christ's body cannot reap the benefits of his or her union with the other members of the body, nor can that member serve the other members of the body. We function best in Christ's body when we function together, gathered around the means of grace.

Q: Is a synod a church in the same sense that our local congregation can be called a church?

A: God has given to his New Testament church wonderful gospel freedom in how we organize ourselves to carry out the work he has given us to do. He has entrusted every Christian with the gospel (1 Peter 2:9) and has called us to work together to carry that gospel to the ends of the earth. And he has made us a beautiful promise as we gather in his name to do that work: "Where two or three come together in my name, there am I with them" (Matthew 18:20). Nowhere in Scripture does Jesus add any organizational conditions that must exist for this promise to be true. In whatever way Christians gather to do the work Jesus gave us to do, we possess the keys of the kingdom Christ has given us and can trust Christ's special promise to be with us. Whenever two or more Christians gather in Jesus' name to carry out Jesus' work, we are the church in the truest sense of the word, that is, a gathering of believers. Christians are gathered as the church whether two or three are found in a local congregation, a national synod, or some other grouping of Christians, such as a Lutheran high school federation.

Wherever believers gather with other believers for the purpose of carrying out some portion of the mission that Christ has given us, there we gather as the church. While it is true that the local congregation will be the most common place for believers to gather to carry out the most comprehensive work of the gospel, that does not make the local congregation any more the *church* than a synod or any other similar gathering of Christians in the name of Jesus. In every age and in every place, God has given gospel freedom to his believers to organize the worldwide work of spreading the gospel in whatever way best serves the gospel in that time and place.

Why are we so careful to state that visible gatherings of believers bear the name church "only because of the true believers present in them"?

A: We are careful that we don't associate the concept of church in its biblical sense with some outward visible structure or grouping of people. No one will enter heaven merely because of an affiliation with a particular congregation or synod no matter how faithful to the Word that congregation or synod showed itself to be.

5. We believe that God directs believers to acknowledge oneness in faith with Christians whose confession of faith submits to all the teachings of Scripture (John 8:31; 1 Thessalonians 5:21,22). We believe, furthermore, that individuals through their membership in a church body commit themselves to the doctrine and practice of that church. To assert that unity exists where there is no agreement in confession is to presume to look into people's hearts. Only God can look into people's hearts. It is not necessary that all Christians agree on matters of church ritual or organization. About these the New Testament gives no commands (Romans 14:17).

Q: Since it is faith in Jesus that saves, why is it so important to hold to all the teachings of Scripture?

A: Every word breathed by the Holy Spirit is important. We believe Scripture is inspired by God himself and reveals to us what God wants us to know. "From infancy you have known the holy Scriptures, which are able to make you wise for salvation through faith in Christ Jesus. All Scripture is God-breathed and is useful for teaching, rebuking, correcting and training in righteousness, so that the man of God may be thoroughly equipped for every good work" (2 Timothy 3:15-17). For us to claim that there are portions of what the Spirit inspired that we can discard with no loss is to claim a greater wisdom than the Spirit. We may not even always realize the importance to our faith of each and every portion of God's Word. What we discard as unimportant may have an importance far beyond anything we realize. Rather than looking for reasons to discard various portions of the Bible as unimportant, we adopt the attitude of the psalm writer who said, "I have not departed from your laws, for you yourself have taught me. How sweet are your words to my taste, sweeter than honey to my mouth! I gain understanding from your precepts; therefore I hate every wrong path" (Psalm 119:102-104).

Q: What is church fellowship?

A: While the invisible fellowship of the holy Christian church always exists because there is but one body of Christ, God would also have us seek to work together visibly with fellow Christians for the sake of the advancement of the truth of the gospel. Wherever Christians outwardly work together to accomplish the work Christ has given his church to do, that is the practice of church fellowship. Perhaps the simplest and most beautiful definition of church fellowship found in Scripture is in 3 John. There, after commending a Christian by the name of Gaius for welcoming into his home some traveling preachers of the truth of the gospel, John writes, "We ought therefore to show hospitality to such men so that we may work together for the truth" (3 John 8). Such working together for the sake of the truth of the gospel is a proper expression of church fellowship.

Obviously, there is also another side to church fellowship. Where disagreement persists on what exactly is the truth of the gospel, Christians cannot work together "for the truth." Then working together could only cause confusion or compromise about what the true message of the gospel really is. Wherever outwardly working together in the kingdom, that is, church fellowship, would give the impression that differences in teachings don't really matter, then our working together is no longer "for the truth." Where Christians do not agree on all the doctrines of God's Word, our working together would only seem to indicate that differences in teachings are unimportant and that God's truth is a matter open to debate. Agreement on God's truth is the basis on which we enjoy the blessings of outward church fellowship. Paul made that clear in Romans 16:17: "I urge you, brothers, to watch out for those who cause divisions and put obstacles in your way that are contrary to the teaching you have learned. Keep away from them." The psalmist reminds us, "I gain understanding from your precepts; therefore I hate every wrong path" (Psalm 119:104). To "hate every wrong path" and yet to cooperate with those who have taken those paths in their teachings pursues neither truth nor love.

Q: **Why would it be judging hearts to establish church fellowship on the basis of someone's personal faith instead of his or her church membership?**

A: By membership in a church, a person is declaring agreement with the teachings of that church. Church membership is a public statement that anyone can see and judge by the Word of God. We would be calling a person insincere if we did not accept at face value his or her public confession of membership. If the church body to which some belong teaches false doctrine, then they subscribe to it because of their membership.

Some people may disagree with the teachings of their churches. For those who proclaim faithfulness to the truth of

Scripture in disagreement with their churches, we would urge them to witness to that truth within their churches. When that witness is ignored, we would urge those Christians to separate themselves from the congregations that are ignoring their witness to the truth. To continue to remain in a church where one is convinced that the truth of the Word is compromised is incompatible with Christian faith and with the desire to make a clear witness to the truth of God.

Q: What are some examples of "matters of church ritual or organization" about which congregations do not need to agree?

A: Even within our own synod, not all congregations follow exactly the same liturgical forms of worship as all others. Other congregations have variations in their church councils, boards, and committees. Many congregations operate Lutheran elementary schools; most do not. God has directed us to be faithful to all of his Word. But in many areas of congregational life, God has given us great freedom. We may organize ourselves for the mission he has given us in the ways that best meet the opportunities for spreading the gospel in each of our congregation's settings.

Q: Why wouldn't we join in fellowship with a person from a different church body who clearly disagreed with the false teachings in his or her church?

A: As long as someone still holds membership in a church, that believer subscribes to that church's teaching. Certainly we would encourage a Christian belonging to a church that teaches false doctrine to witness to the truth to leaders and others within that congregation. Where that witness is clearly ignored, we would then urge that Christian to witness to the truth by separating from those who persist in the false teachings. At that time we would urge that believer to join his or her witness to ours so that we might indeed work together for the truth.

6. We believe that those whose confession of faith reveals that they are united in the doctrines of Scripture will express their fellowship in Christ as occasion permits (Ephesians 4:3). They may express their fellowship by joint worship, by joint proclamation of the gospel, by joining in Holy Communion, by joint prayer, and by joint church work. God directs believers not to practice religious fellowship with those whose confession and actions reveal that they teach, tolerate, support, or defend error (2 John 10,11). When error appears in the church, Christians will try to preserve their fellowship by patiently admonishing the offenders, in the hope that they will turn from their error (2 Timothy 2:25,26; Titus 3:10). But the Lord commands believers not to practice church fellowship with people who persist in teaching or adhering to beliefs that are false (Romans 16:17,18).

Q: How long are we to go on admonishing someone who is holding to a false teaching before we break fellowship with him or her?

A: We must remember to admonish in the spirit of our Savior, with humility and love. We patiently warn and correct as long as we are convinced that the person is willing to listen and as long as we believe that there is a chance the person will turn away from the false teaching. Believers always keep in mind God's concern for individual souls. The prophet Isaiah expressed it: "A bruised reed he will not break, and a smoldering wick he will not snuff out" (42:3). Paul also suggests the proper attitude for the faithful shepherd of the flock and any Christian: "Those who oppose him he must gently instruct, in the hope that God will grant them repentance leading them to a knowledge of the truth" (2 Timothy 2:25).

But it is quite another matter if that person refuses to listen and shows no willingness to change. Sometimes that means that the one holding to the false teaching seeks to win others to those false views. Then we are no longer dealing with a believer who has wandered from the truth at a time of weakness or temptation. Instead that person endangers others by seeking to convince others of his or her opinion. Others may become confused by the opinions they hear from that person. At that point, love for souls cannot delay. When someone has begun to play the role of a divider within a congregation of believers, then Paul's words to Titus come into play: "Warn a divisive person once, and then warn him a second time. After that, have nothing to do with him" (Titus 3:10).

 Since every Christian often struggles with misunderstandings or doubts about Scripture, why doesn't that make it impossible to have fellowship with anyone?

A: Struggling with misunderstandings and doubts troubles all Christians until the day they are home in heaven. Struggling with misunderstandings and doubts does not end church fellowship but is a reason to practice our fellowship with other believers in order to encourage one another through the Word to more firmly grasp God's truth. Believers should have the spirit of Samuel before the Word of our God:

"Speak, for your servant is listening" (1 Samuel 3:10). Our fellowship is not broken by misunderstandings and doubts but by unwillingness to listen to God's truth and determined persistence to cling to false doctrine.

Q: How can we correct and encourage someone else when we ourselves struggle with doubts and misunderstandings all the time?

A: Yes, every Christian will struggle with doubts and misunderstandings. But the Scripture repeatedly warns about false teachings and encourages believers to remain faithful to the truth. Church fellowship is not about any individual's perfect knowledge of Scripture; rather, it is the conviction that Scripture's doctrines are clear and that the Bible does not contradict itself in any of its teachings. Church fellowship is about allowing Scripture to speak without allowing human reason to take anything away from what it teaches or to add anything to its teachings. Church fellowship is really a testimony to the fact that God's inspired Word is clear enough to lead us to an understanding of everything that it shares with us.

Q: Why do we separate from a church body that shares almost all the same teachings with us?

A: When we separate from a church body that shares almost all the same teachings, we know that many Christians are within that church body. It continues to be a Christian denomination where the gospel creates and nourishes faith. But false doctrine spreads like gangrene (2 Timothy 2:17) and will endanger faith if ignored. Out of love for the believers in other denominations, we desire to warn them of the danger. God gives us the responsibility to separate (Romans 16:17) and speak what we believe. If we do not warn others, we allow them to endanger their faith.

We must remain faithful to God as well. God has revealed his truth to us in Scripture, and we cannot give the impression that any teaching of God's Word is superfluous or unimportant. When we continue to practice church fellowship with those who teach something false, we allow opposing doctrines to be defended and taught side by side. This suggests either that God must have failed in clearly inspiring his Word or that perhaps there are contradictions and errors in that Word. God asks us to confess the truth and hold to the teaching of Jesus (John 8:31). It is the Word of God that makes us wise for salvation and equips us for every good work (2 Timothy 3:15-17). We desire to be faithful to Jesus.

We still recognize such churches as Christian and thankfully acknowledge that many Christians are within their fellowship, yet where there is persistent disagreement over teachings of Scripture, we cannot work together for the truth. We must continue to use every opportunity God gives us to solve those differences in doctrine so that we can establish or reestablish true fellowship.

Q: What does it mean for me to "avoid" those who teach false doctrine?

A: Every Christian has contact with believers and unbelievers every day. Every friend of a Christian may not be Christian. In our day-to-day lives, God does not want us to isolate ourselves from everyone who believes differently. We do not avoid social, business, and personal contact with others. Instead we are to use our contact with others to share our faith and let our light shine (Matthew 5:16).

But God wants us to be careful about our religious contact with others. Christians express their faith and confess their unity with others when they worship, pray, attend Holy Communion, and work together to do the Lord's work. We are to avoid doing these things with those who do not believe as we do. Christians desire to work together for the truth with those who share a common faith in what the truth is. Agreeing to disagree is an offense to the clarity of God's perfect Word. Expressing our faith together with those who do not share a common faith suggests that differences in faith don't matter.

Q: How can I confess the truth when I must be in a church that is not of our fellowship?

A: From time to time, a Christian must attend a worship service in a church that teaches differently. Sometimes family obligations or friendships require us to attend such services. The goal of the whole doctrine of church fellowship is to give a clear and loving testimony to our faith that all the truth of God's Word matters. We do not want to give the impression that the false teaching of that church body is unimportant. But we recognize that wherever the gospel is proclaimed, the Holy Spirit will create believers and nourish their faith. We do not want to disturb their worship, even though we cannot join with them in their worship. Maintaining respectful silence during the prayers and hymns and sitting quietly while they receive Holy Communion are ways to give a quiet testimony to the truth of the gospel. It is good also to be ready to give a testimony that patiently and in all humility explains your actions should someone notice and ask you for an explanation.

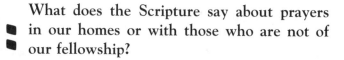

Q: What does the Scripture say about prayers in our homes or with those who are not of our fellowship?

A: Scripture is not a rule book that promises to give us directions in every situation. Rather, Scripture gives us basic principles and the power of the gospel to apply them in Christian love.

The very same principles that apply between church bodies apply also between individual Christians. Simply, a Christian does not want to act in any way or say anything that would indicate that any truth of Scripture is unimportant. Whenever truth of Scripture is persistently denied and rejected, joint prayers would not confess the truth of all the Word of God. Instead the prayers would imply that the differences between truth and false doctrine could be overlooked.

But having guests in our own home does not mean we must refrain from speaking our regular prayers at the table or conducting our routine devotions. When we have guests in our church, we do not refrain from speaking our public prayers, singing our hymns, or preaching the gospel. The apostle Paul offered up his prayer in the presence of those on the ship with him (Acts 27:35). Many of them did not believe as he did. To omit prayers may cause more confusion and provide an unclear witness. We may not ask them to join us in our prayer. At such times we can simply speak as we would as if we were alone in our home.

At times those in our home may confess their faith in Jesus alone and by their testimony clearly reveal that they do not share or understand the false teachings of their church. We would rejoice at that confession and join with them in prayer. In fact, at such times, refusing to pray with a weak brother or sister might do more harm than good.

At other times, we might be present in situations that involve matters of life and death. Then Christian love moves us to encourage, comfort, and pray with those facing such trauma or difficulty. God places us in those situations to share our faith and the hope and comfort we have in Christ. Christian love makes room for the possibility of exceptional cases. Yet exceptions do not change the basic principles.

Q: ▪ Doesn't separating ourselves from others
▪ only make clear what we are against?

A: ▪ Some do perceive the practice of church fellowship in
negative terms, what we are against. But there are two reasons to
look beyond that perception. First, the apostle John wrote, "It
gave me great joy to have some brothers come and tell about your
faithfulness to the truth and how you continue to walk in the
truth. I have no greater joy than to hear that my children are
walking in the truth" (3 John 3,4). The doctrine of fellowship
celebrates the work of the Holy Spirit in bringing believers
together who share the same truth. We can find great joy in working together with those who are "walking in the truth." Christians are always saddened when they must separate from those
who no longer share the same truth. Church fellowship permits
us to work to preserve and nurture genuine unity in the truth.

Second, we apply the doctrine of fellowship not because of
what we are against but because of what we are for. We are for
the truth of all the Word because we are convinced that the
truth of the Scriptures is what makes us wise for salvation and
equips us for every good work. We are for faithful testimony to
the alone saving gospel of Jesus Christ.

---

7. We believe that every Christian is a priest before
God (1 Peter 2:9). All believers have direct and equal
access to the throne of grace through Christ, the mediator (Ephesians 2:17,18). God has given the means of
grace to all believers. All Christians are to declare the
praises of him who called them out of darkness into his
wonderful light (1 Peter 2:9). In this sense all Christians
are ministers, or servants, of the gospel. God wants all
Christians to share the message of salvation with other
people (Matthew 28:19,20; 10:32).

Q: When do Christians become priests of God?

A: Our *ordination* into God's royal priesthood is in the water of our baptism. As Peter tells us, everyone who has been built onto the cornerstone of Jesus can be given these names: "You are a chosen people, a royal priesthood, a holy nation, a people belonging to God, that you may declare the praises of him who called you out of darkness into his wonderful light" (1 Peter 2:9). One of the reasons Lutherans refrain from using the title "priest" to speak of those in the public ministry is that it obscures the beautiful truth that all Christians are part of "a royal priesthood" from the moment they are brought to faith.

Q: Where has God called Christians to carry out their priesthood?

A: The "royal priesthood" is the real vocation for the life of every Christian; we carry out our priesthood in every activity of life in which we express our faith. "Therefore, I urge you, brothers, in view of God's mercy, to offer your bodies as living sacrifices, holy and pleasing to God—this is your spiritual act of worship" (Romans 12:1). Opportunities to offer such "sacrifices" as Christ's "royal priesthood" are found wherever we are. In fact, the entire life of a believer presents opportunities to offer beautiful sacrifices to God.

For example, when we carry out our jobs faithfully and honestly, we are offering a priestly sacrifice "holy and pleasing to God." When we love and care for our families, we offer a beautiful sacrifice as part of "a royal priesthood." Whenever we seize the opportunities God gives us to "give the reason for the hope that [we] have" (1 Peter 3:15), we are again offering up sacrifices that in Christ are a delight to our Lord.

For believers in Christ, no division between the sacred and secular applies to their lives of service. Believers encourage and live for others in their congregations, but they also live for others and honor their Savior at work and when they relax. Believers are priests of God at all times.

Q: Since we all have direct access to God's throne of grace, why do we at times ask other Christians to pray for us in church or in their private prayers?

A: Certainly each believer in Christ has full access to the throne of God and the full promise to be heard and answered because of Jesus. It's not as though our prayers have no power unless we join them to the prayers of another Christian. But Jesus himself speaks of combining our prayers with the prayers of others: "Again, I tell you that if two of you on earth agree about anything you ask for, it will be done for you by my Father in heaven" (Matthew 18:19). Jesus does not forbid us to come alone to the throne of grace. But he does suggest that believers can ask another Christian or many Christians to pray together.

Q: How can all Christians be called ministers?

A: The essential meaning of the word *minister* is "servant" or "slave." When we consider that all Christians are servants of Christ, we can say that all are servants and, therefore, all are ministers. On the other hand, not all Christians are called to exercise their service or ministry publicly for others as full-time church workers. We have traditionally used the term *minister* to refer to those called servants. But it is not incorrect to call all Christians ministers in the sense that they serve Jesus and others in their daily activities.

8. We believe that God has also established the public ministry of the Word (Ephesians 4:11), and it is the will of God that the church, in accordance with good order (1 Corinthians 14:40), call qualified individuals into this public ministry (1 Timothy 3:1-10; 1 Corinthians 9:14). Such individuals minister publicly, that is, not because as individuals they possess the universal priesthood but because they are asked to do this in the name of fellow Christians (Romans 10:15). These individuals are the called servants of Christ and ministers of the gospel. They are not to be lords over God's church (1 Peter 5:3). We believe that when the church calls individuals into this public ministry, the Lord himself is acting through the church (Acts 20:28). We believe that the church has the freedom to establish various forms within the one ministry of the Word, such as pastors, Christian teachers, and staff ministers. Through its call, the church in Christian liberty designates the place and scope of service.

Q: What is the difference between the priesthood of all believers and the public ministry?

A: The priesthood of all believers is the privilege and right that all believers possess to proclaim the gospel of Jesus Christ, approach the throne of grace in prayer, and praise God with no other mediator than Jesus Christ. Believers carry out that priesthood privately in their daily lives with fellow Christians and with all people.

Yet Jesus has also instituted the public ministry, or representative ministry, of the gospel. He permits groups of believers to call in a public way those who will serve them with the gospel. For example, since not all have the gifts, abilities, or qualifications to preach publicly, believers call someone to do that for them, a pastor. Whenever any group of priests or believers asks another believer to serve them in the gospel, then that believer is called and serves in the public, or representative, ministry.

Q: **Why has God established the public ministry when all Christians are priests entrusted with sharing the gospel?**

A: There are two basic reasons why God has established the public ministry. First, God desires individuals to serve as spiritual shepherds to watch over the souls of other believers, warning and encouraging them in the faith with God's law and gospel. While all Christians have been entrusted with the gospel, God calls some to be these special watchmen (Ezekiel 33) for the spiritual welfare of his people. Paul reminded the elders of Ephesus of that task of the public ministry when he said, "Keep watch over yourselves and all the flock of which the Holy Spirit has made you overseers. Be shepherds of the church of God, which he bought with his own blood" (Acts 20:28).

Second, those in the public ministry work to train and equip others through the Word for service as God's royal priests. Paul points out that purpose for the public ministry in Ephesians 4: "It was [Christ] who gave some to be apostles, some to be prophets, some to be evangelists, and some to be pastors and teachers, to prepare God's people for works of service, so that the body of Christ may be built up" (verses 11,12). In this way, the public ministry doesn't replace the priesthood of all believers; rather, the public ministry serves as God's tool to enable us to live out our priesthood in daily life.

Q: Public ministers are not lords over Christ's flock. Why do we give them honor and obedience?

A: Which side of the issue we emphasize depends on the position in which God has placed us. If we are being served by those in the public ministry, we need to take to heart the truth that God does urge his people to honor those who serve them in the public ministry. In 1 Timothy 5:17 we are reminded, "The elders who direct the affairs of the church well are worthy of double honor, especially those whose work is preaching and teaching." Also in Hebrews 13:17 we are told, "Obey your leaders and submit to their authority. They keep watch over you as men who must give an account. Obey them so that their work will be a joy, not a burden, for that would be of no advantage to you." How important that we remember that those called into the public ministry are representatives of Christ.

On the other side, God urges his public ministers to humble service. Public ministry is not a status but an opportunity. Peter wrote, "Be shepherds of God's flock that is under your care, serving as overseers—not because you must, but because you are willing, as God wants you to be; not greedy for money, but eager to serve; not lording it over those entrusted to you, but being examples to the flock" (1 Peter 5:2,3). Those who represent Christ should remember the attitude of the Savior who "did not come to be served, but to serve" (Matthew 20:28).

Q: Why does our church body follow the procedure we do when calling public ministers?

A: The apostle Paul asks this question in Romans 10:15: "How can they preach unless they are sent?" No one is to take the public ministry upon himself. Since all Christians are royal priests of God who have been entrusted with the gospel, no royal priest of God has the right to place himself in a position of authority or responsibility over other royal priests of God unless asked. Therefore, a group of Christians issues a call to someone to serve them. That is nothing more or less than God's people asking a believer to serve them with the gospel.

At special times, God called his public ministers directly with no human intermediaries. For example, Jesus directly called his apostles during his earthly ministry. The church has given the label "immediate call" to such direct calls by God. But today God's usual way of calling someone into the public ministry is through a mediate call. Simply, instead of calling directly, God calls through the means of his royal priests who ask someone to serve them in the public ministry. Every gathering of believers has the right, in Jesus' name, to entrust specific duties of the gospel ministry to those whom they call to serve them. In this way, Jesus continues to bless his church with those who serve and equip his people.

Exactly how a congregation or church body goes about this calling procedure is a matter agreed upon in brotherly love. Scripture has not set any steps for the procedure other than urging us to carry out the Lord's work "in a fitting and orderly way" (1 Corinthians 14:40). The goal of any calling procedure is that both those serving in the public ministry and those being served are certain that a valid call into the ministry has been given. Such a valid call assures both those serving and those being served that the call into the ministry has really been issued by God himself through his people.

Q: Where in Scripture does it say that we are given the freedom to establish various forms of the public ministry?

A: In the Old Testament church, God gave the ceremonial law that governed his people's worship life. God has not given any similar laws to his New Testament church. Great freedom marks how the church is to carry out its work to advance the cause of the gospel. The public ministry was clearly instituted by Jesus (Ephesians 4:10-12) and the qualifications for those who would serve in such positions of responsibility are set down in Scripture (1 Timothy 3). Yet nowhere do the Scriptures of the New Testament define or prescribe specific job descriptions for all places and all times for those serving in the New Testament public ministry. The early Christians in Jerusalem provide an example of Christian freedom in establishing forms of public ministry. They chose to call seven men to help carry out the ministry and designated the scope of their calls (Acts 6).

Q: Is such freedom necessary?

A: God has given his New Testament church such gospel freedom to form and shape specific positions within the public ministry to meet the unique needs and challenges of every age. This freedom gives the church great flexibility in shaping the forms of the public ministry, and it allows the church to adjust as it carries out the mission of sharing the gospel. It is fascinating to see how the early church used such freedom of form in the public ministry as it responded to specific needs at specific times. When ministry demands in Jerusalem were threatening to take the apostles' focus off the Word of God and prayer, the congregation at Jerusalem established a new position of service (Acts 6). Directed by God, the church in Antioch sent away two of their spiritual leaders to be world missionaries (Acts 13).

We have such examples today. Confronted with the challenges of family life with which many Christians struggle, some congregations have established a position of family minister.

His chief work is to apply the Word to family life in order to instruct, encourage, and strengthen families to carry out the spiritual nurture of all those in the home. In every age, the church has such freedom to meet specific needs with specific forms of the gospel ministry.

9. We believe that the church's mission is to serve people with the Word and sacraments. This service is usually done in local congregations. We look upon the pastoral office as the most comprehensive form of the public ministry of the Word. Pastors are trained and called to provide such comprehensive spiritual oversight for the gathering and nurturing of souls in congregations (1 Peter 5:2).

Q: How is the pastoral office the most comprehensive form of the public ministry?

A: The work of any form of the public ministry is determined by the scope, that is, the specific tasks, of the call that is issued by the royal priests, or believers. When we say that the pastor's call is the most comprehensive form of the public ministry, we simply mean that the tasks expected of the pastor are the broadest within the church. The work of a Lutheran elementary school teacher is more narrowly defined with special emphasis on one age group—even specifying one classroom as the primary field of work. The pastor's call most often deals with caring for the spiritual needs of all the different ages in the congregation. He is entrusted with the public proclamation of the gospel and the distribution of the sacraments for the spiritual welfare of all within his congregation. In these and other ways, his call has a breadth that is greater than that of other forms of the public ministry.

Q: ■ **Why is the Christian congregation the most basic form of the visible church?**

A: Every gathering in the name of Jesus to do the work of the gospel is a congregation with the promise of his special presence and blessing (Matthew 18:20). Such congregations may be gatherings of Christians on a local, regional, or national basis. However, it is certainly true that most often when Christians gather together it will be in a congregation of believers that is local. It is also true that the vast majority of the work of the gospel in the daily life of God's people takes place within the local congregation. In such ways, the local congregation serves as the most basic form of the visible gathering of the church.

Q: **Why do pastors need many years of training?**

A: A loving pastoral heart, patterned after the Savior's humble compassion, is a key qualification for the ministry. But a pastor should also have a knowledge of history that will help him understand not only what has happened in the Christian church but also in the world. He should also be able to express his thoughts clearly and understand the ideas and expressions of others. He should have some knowledge of literature so that he can communicate not just with believers but also with those outside the church. In other words, a pastor should be an educated man who is able to communicate the gospel clearly.

We want our pastors to "correctly [handle] the word of truth" (2 Timothy 2:15). In order to ensure that as best as we can, we require pastoral candidates to spend years of intense study to learn the original languages of Scripture. Such learning of the original languages of the Bible enables them to publicly preach and teach with absolute confidence: "This is what the Lord says." It is a rich blessing to our congregations that pastors can mine the truth of the Word for themselves instead of relying on the strengths and weaknesses of a Bible translation or the insights of Bible commentators. Having well-trained pastors is a time-consuming and expensive process, but not as expensive for the kingdom as having poorly trained shepherds.

The long pastoral training course helps candidates for the pastoral ministry to develop the skills needed for their work. Just as we want our doctors to have both compassion and skill, so too we desire that combination of gifts in those who, as Christ's servants, serve as physicians of our souls. The same encouragement that Paul gave to young Timothy applies today: "Do your best to present yourself to God as one approved, a workman who does not need to be ashamed and who correctly handles the word of truth" (2 Timothy 2:15).

10. We believe that women may participate in offices and activities of the public ministry except where that work involves authority over men (1 Timothy 2:11,12). This means that women may not serve as pastors nor participate in assemblies of the church in ways that exercise authority over men (1 Corinthians 11:3; 14:33-35).

Q: Why do we limit how women serve in public ministry?

A: If those we call into the public ministry were called according to a set of requirements that we have set up, then we would have no right to limit who serves in the public ministry. But not only is the public ministry God's gift to his church; those who serve in public ministry and how they serve are parts of God's plan as well. While both men and women can and do serve in the public ministry in our midst, such service cannot be done in any way that would violate another principle of God's Word. We cannot ignore what Scripture has to say about the complementary roles God has given to women and men in his world. We simply cannot ignore the words from the inspired pen of the apostle Paul: "I do not permit a woman to teach or to have authority over a man; she must be silent" (1 Timothy 2:12). No matter what gifts for the public ministry God has given to a person, man or woman, those gifts can only be used as blessings for God's church when they are used as God's Word directs them to be used.

Q: Why do we say that if women would vote in the church, it would be exercising authority over a man? Wouldn't that simply be exercising authority alongside the men of the congregation?

A: The basic principle in exercising our God-given roles as women and men is what Paul stated in 1 Timothy 2:12, "I do not permit a woman to teach or to have authority over a man." Not all voting in a congregation is an exercise of authority, but for women to participate in any vote that exercises authority over men would be a violation of the scriptural principle. The voters' assemblies of our congregations typically have the right to call or elect and remove the called workers and lay leaders of the congregation. In addition, voters' assemblies pass resolutions involving the acceptance and removal of members, including the final step of love that declares a former brother or sister in Christ to be outside the kingdom of God. We believe such voting is an exercise of the authority of the keys that Christ has entrusted to his church. Since the voters of the congregation have been entrusted with that authority, it would be a violation of the principle of headship to allow both the men and the women of the congregation to vote in such congregational meetings.

 How do single women and widows express their views on congregational issues when they do not have men from their households to speak for them?

A: The debt of Christian love to one another makes it imperative that a congregation seek out ways to hear the concerns and ideas of the single women and widows within the congregation. Some congregations have solved this problem by holding open forums where information about the congregation's ministry is disseminated and questions and ideas are shared. Thorough communication through other means and an open-door policy by all called, elected, or appointed leaders can also help make sure that the needs and concerns of all of the members are heard. In the congregation of Jerusalem (Acts 6), the concerns of the women were heard and acted upon.

Q: **If women have equal access to the throne of God as priests of God, doesn't that imply equal authority in the church as well?**

A: We must be careful that we don't set one teaching of God's Word (the priesthood of all believers) against another teaching of his Word (the God-ordained and unique roles of men and women). We might think these ideas are in apposition to one another rather than in harmony. In many places in Scripture, men and women carry out the exact same functions as priests of God. For example, Aquila and his wife, Priscilla, together in the privacy of their home helped Apollos understand God's truth more adequately (Acts 18:26). Yet God has also clearly indicated that when exercising Christ's authority in his church over a mixed group of men and women, the unique roles given to men and women should not be ignored. We should not presume to know more than God whenever we cannot understand his will. Rather, we should humbly recognize our own human limitations and God's boundless wisdom. He has given us all things in Christ (Romans 8:31,32), and he has revealed nothing to us that will harm us.

11. We reject any attempt to identify the holy Christian church with an outward organization. We reject any claim that the church must function in the world through specific organizational forms.

Q: **Do we believe that the WELS is the same as the holy Christian church?**

A: No. We clearly teach the difference between visible gatherings of believers and the invisible holy Christian church. We believe that everything our church teaches is in line with Scripture. But that does not imply that Christians do not exist in any denomination other than our own. Such an idea confuses a visible gathering of believers with the whole holy Christian church. Although any false doctrine is always a deadly danger to faith, because of the power of the Spirit in the gospel there are members of the holy Christian church wherever the gospel is heard. Such believers will be found both in orthodox (true teaching) and heterodox (false teaching) visible church bodies. While we will want to outwardly fellowship with those whom we are convinced share a common outward confession of all the truth, we will also joyfully confess, as we do in the Nicene Creed, that "we believe in one holy Christian and apostolic Church." The body of Christ is not divided along any denominational lines. In all Christian church bodies, "the Lord knows those who are his" (2 Timothy 2:19).

12. We reject as false ecumenicity any views that look for the true unity of the church in some form of external or organizational union, and we oppose all movements toward such union made at the expense of a clear confession of all the teachings of Scripture. We reject the contention that religious fellowship may be practiced without agreement in doctrine and practice. There must be agreement in the confession of scriptural doctrines, and also one's actions or practice must show that error is not tolerated.

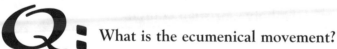

Q: What is the ecumenical movement?

A: The ecumenical movement is a worldwide effort within the visible Christian church to unite the visible Christian church either by merging denominations or by agreeing to join in full fellowship across denominational lines. In certain instances, some in the ecumenical movement have even sought ways to express common beliefs with other world religions beyond Christianity.

Q: Isn't uniting all Christians a noble task?

A: The struggle for true outward unity among Christians is a very noble task. In his great High Priestly Prayer, our Savior himself asked his Father, "May they be brought to complete unity to let the world know that you sent me and have loved them even as you have loved me" (John 17:23). True outward unity among Christians would send a powerful witness to the world of the love of Christ we profess. In contrast, the disunity and divisions that have plagued the church over the centuries are an offense to the unbelieving world. The less the visible church reflects the true unity of the invisible body of Christ the greater is that offense. Every Christian will want to make use of every opportunity to undo such offense by seeking to preserve true visible unity where it exists and to restore it where it is now lacking.

But only one source of true unity exists. Jesus states that quite simply in John 8:31,32 where he says, "If you hold to my teaching, you are really my disciples. Then you will know the truth, and the truth will set you free." Visible unity gained at the expense of a mangled confession of the saving truth of Scripture is an ugly distortion of the true spiritual unity about which Jesus spoke in his prayer. Nowhere does our Savior give us the right to seek to gain outward unity by ignoring portions of God's Word. Any unity gained by doctrinal compromise would yield only a large earthly organization whose testimony to the world would be a jumbled distortion of the saving gospel. The real goal of outward unity among Christians is to impress on the world the power of the truth of the gospel, not to impress the world with the size of our organization.

A spirit of doctrinal compromise and indifference is often clearly visible in much of the ecumenical movement. The authority and verbal inspiration of Scripture and many other doctrines are considered minor details that should not stand in the way of the greater good of unity. Many involved in the ecumenical movement believe that church bodies can simply agree to disagree on the details of doctrine while they move ahead in practicing full outward fellowship.

The goal of outward unity is a noble task, but the chosen path of doctrinal compromise distorts an otherwise noble desire for the visible unity among Christians. Such a zeal for outward unity at all costs fails to take into account the many warnings of Scripture about the danger of false doctrine. As Paul once warned Timothy, "For the time will come when men will not put up with sound doctrine. Instead, to suit their own desires, they will gather around them a great number of teachers to say what their itching ears want to hear" (2 Timothy 4:3).

Q: What would be wrong with basing the amount of working together between churches on the degree of agreement between teachings?

A: Such an outward fellowship based on most or some doctrines presumes to be able to know which doctrines of Scripture are more important and which are less important. It presumes that we can rank the inspired truths of God from greatest to least, with differences in some doctrines being divisive and others not necessarily being completely divisive. Nowhere does Scripture propose such a ranking to us. In fact, consider Jesus' strong warning in Matthew 5:19 for anyone who would dare to alter what might be considered "the least of these commandments."

In addition, such a ranking of doctrines is a thorough confusion of the visible and invisible churches. It is true that what saves us is only faith in the absolute perfection of the life and death of the eternal Son of God made flesh for us (the true invisible fellowship of the church). However, that does not mean that by our practice of outward fellowship we give the impression that clinging to any "lesser" false doctrine is relatively unimportant. "Everything that was written in the past was written to teach us" (Romans 15:4). Nowhere does Scripture give to our human reason the right to sit in judgment on what God has revealed. We cannot render human judgments about which false doctrines must only partially divide us outwardly and which false doctrines must completely divide us. Such "rules taught by men" (Matthew 15:9) lead only to greater and greater indifference about all doctrine.

False doctrine is poison for the soul. To deal carelessly with false doctrine by engaging in a form of outward fellowship where any such poison is preached and practiced risks the spiritual death of Christians. When Jesus warned us about false prophets and labeled them "ferocious wolves" despite their coming to us in "sheep's clothing" (Matthew 7:15), he wasn't urging his sheep to hang around some "wolves" while moving away from other "wolves" whom they perceived, by some self-chosen standard, to be a little less "ferocious." While we know that God can preserve faith even among false prophets and those who follow them, Scripture teaches us only one standard to determine outward visible fellowship: all the truths of Scripture.

Q **: Why is it important to agree in doctrine *and* practice?**

A **:** If agreement in doctrine is as thin as the paper it is written on, there is really no agreement. If the truth is confessed in writing but not consistently practiced and preached in the life of the church, such agreement in doctrine is meaningless. We know that this side of heaven no Christian will ever perfectly live or practice what he or she claims to believe, but a willingness to be corrected by the clear Word of God gives evidence that real agreement in doctrine and practice does indeed exist.

13. We reject participation or membership in organizations that have religious features in conflict with the Christian faith, such as most lodges.

Q: When should we avoid membership in an organization or group?

A: We are redeemed by the blood of Jesus. God declares us free of sin because of Jesus, and we claim that acquittal by faith. The Scripture reminds us that this is all by grace through faith and that we do not earn it by our behavior (Ephesians 2:8,9).

Many organizations seek to benefit society by helping children, the disabled, the poor, and others. Believers desire to help remove suffering, discrimination, poverty, and hunger and to join with others to work for humanitarian goals. Sometimes, however, organizations move away from purely humanitarian relief by incorporating religious principles that suggest that our deeds win God's approval and involving prayers that eliminate Jesus. Believers in Jesus would oppose such approaches and would avoid distorting the work of Jesus in redeeming us. Where religious principles become a part of the goals and purposes of an organization, we would avoid it and find another outlet for our concern and compassion for others.

In some organizations, spiritual or religious aspects are not part of their goals and purposes. Instead they are clearly devoted to social or business concerns. A prayer at the beginning of the meeting may be the only "spiritual" aspect of the group. In such circumstances, a believer will participate in the social, humanitarian, or business function and ask the leadership to change a religious practice that is outside the goals of the group or to respect his or her desire not to participate in that religious aspect. Our concern is always that we don't give the impression that we are working together for the truth of the gospel where there is no agreement on what that truth is. Since the purposes and organization of groups can change rapidly, we will always want to be vigilant about what "confession" our membership in any organization is making.

Q: Where in Scripture does it warn of such associations?

A: Every passage that warns us about compromising the truth and failing to discern false doctrine applies. The doctrine of fellowship does not give us a set of rules about where we can shop, with whom we can eat, or who can be our friends. Yet love for the truth of the Word leads us to refuse to compromise if any of our associations with others would lead to an implied or explicit denial of the truth of all of God's Word. Wherever our associations in life would place us in a position of seeming to deny the gracious work of Jesus, we must confess Jesus rather than deny him. We would give an unclear testimony about the truth of the gospel by membership in organizations that adopt religious principles different from the Scriptures.

 Why wouldn't it be wise to belong to such an organization for the purpose of gaining an opportunity to witness to the truth?

A: We wouldn't join the Ku Klux Klan in order to testify about the dangers of racial bigotry. Instead we would refuse to join. A refusal to join indicates that we do not share the organization's approach to racial issues. In the same way, we would not participate in any organization that would distort the gospel or the truths of God's Word. Refusing to join indicates that the truths of God's Word are important to us. Such a refusal is a clear witness.

It may happen that an organization to which we already belong suddenly adds a religious requirement to its membership. In such a situation, we can seek to overturn that change for a time. But if the raising of such concerns appears to be fruitless, the most powerful witness would be to explain clearly why we are conscience-bound to end our association with that organization.

Additional Reading for This Section:

Church Fellowship: Working Together for the Truth by John F. Brug

Church—Mission—Ministry: The Family of God by Armin W. Schuetze

Essays on Church Fellowship edited by Curtis A. Jahn

Section VIII.
CHURCH AND STATE

1. We believe that not only the church but also the state, that is, all governmental authority, has been instituted by God. "The authorities that exist have been established by God" (Romans 13:1). Christians will, therefore, for conscience' sake obey the government that rules over them (Romans 13:5) unless that government commands them to disobey God (Acts 5:29).

Q: How can government be an institution of God when so many who govern are not believers who acknowledge the true God?

A: Paul wrote these words to the Christians in Rome: "Everyone must submit himself to the governing authorities, for there is no authority except that which God has established. The authorities that exist have been established by God" (Romans 13:1). At the time, those Christians were under the rule of Emperor Nero. Even a heathen government like that in Rome functioned as God's institution and deserved the honor and respect of the Christians who lived under it. Even the worst government is better than the anarchy and chaos that occurs where people live without the order and protection given by God's gift of government. In fact, an able unbeliever exercising an office in government may prove to be a greater blessing for the Christians living in that society than an unqualified believer.

Q: In what ways can we see God's wisdom in instituting government?

A: Despite all the complaining we so easily do about high taxes or inefficiency in government, we must recognize that government is one of God's greatest blessings for this life. Through our government we receive blessings when we drive on a highway, enjoy the protection of the police department or fire department, and live in peace at home or abroad. All these things, and many more, come through stable government.

Most important, we enjoy religious freedom. In our country we may worship and share our faith without interference from governmental authorities. When God's servants in government are doing their job well, we have many opportunities to do the work of God's kingdom. Paul urges all Christians to pray for those in authority: "I urge, then, first of all, that requests, prayers, intercession and thanksgiving be made for everyone—for kings and all those in authority, that we may live peaceful and quiet lives in all godliness and holiness. This is good, and pleases God our Savior, who wants all men to be saved and to come to a knowledge of the truth" (1 Timothy 2:1-4).

Q: Does the Christian ever have a right to participate in the overthrow of an unjust government?

A: To rebel against a legally established government, even a government that may be unjust and unfair, is to rebel against God. Remember that Paul wrote the great "government" chapter of Scripture, Romans 13, to Christians living under a pagan government that promoted pagan worship. That government would eventually put Paul to death and begin persecutions of other Christians. Nevertheless, Paul wrote about such a government: "The authorities that exist have been established by God. Consequently, he who rebels against the authority is rebelling against what God has instituted, and those who do so will bring judgment on themselves" (Romans 13:1,2).

David is a good example of one who chose to obey rather than rebel. After he was anointed to be the next king of Israel and to rule after the death of King Saul, David did not lead a rebellion. When Saul sought to kill David, David refused to harm Saul, God's anointed king. Even when David had an opportunity to kill Saul, he chose not to harm him. David trusted that God would judge any injustice on Saul's part, but David would not lay a hand on Saul. David proclaimed, "'As surely as the LORD lives,' he said, 'the LORD himself will strike him; either his time will come and he will die, or he will go into battle and perish. But the LORD forbid that I should lay a hand on the LORD's anointed'" (1 Samuel 26:10,11).

Q: **What should we do when our government commands us to do what would be sinful?**

A: We should not sin. Since our government is instituted by God, even it does not have the right to command us to do what God forbids. With the first disciples, we should say to those in authority, "We must obey God rather than men!" (Acts 5:29).

Yet while we will refuse to do the sin our government commands, we will not rebel against our government. There are other options. In a government where the people have a voice, we should protest the law that requires us to sin. We also have the right to leave such a country and find another that would not hinder the living of our faith. Many Christians have fled from such governments over the centuries.

If all else fails, we have the option to suffer the consequences of our conscientious disobedience. The apostles and many other Christians endured punishment for obeying God rather than the government throughout the history of the Christian church. While God does not ask us to seek outward suffering or even martyrdom for our faith, we cannot avoid such things when government law, decree, or policy means denying our Savior. At such times, we hear God's beautiful promise to his children suffering at the hands of their government, "Be faithful, even to the point of death, and I will give you the crown of life" (Revelation 2:10).

Q: What should Christians do if they are convinced that their government is involved in injustice?

A: Even if the injustice does not involve us directly, we cannot remain silent. King Solomon reminds us in the book of Proverbs, "Rescue those being led away to death; hold back those staggering toward slaughter. If you say, 'But we knew nothing about this,' does not he who weighs the heart perceive it? Does not he who guards your life know it?" (24:11,12). And again, "Speak up for those who cannot speak for themselves, for the rights of all who are destitute. Speak up and judge fairly; defend the rights of the poor and needy" (31:8,9). In a government where we have a voice with our representatives, we as individual Christians cannot allow injustice to continue without raising our voices against it. Even if our government will not listen, we can still show mercy and kindness to those who are affected by such injustice. "He who oppresses the poor shows contempt for their Maker, but whoever is kind to the needy honors God" (Proverbs 14:31). Such kindness to those suffering injustice can also give us some wonderful opportunities to witness to the love of Christ that is behind the kindness we show.

2. We believe that God has given the church and the state their own distinct responsibilities. To the church the Lord has assigned the responsibility of calling sinners to repentance, of proclaiming forgiveness through the cross of Christ, and of encouraging believers in their Christian living. The purpose is to lead the elect of God to eternal salvation through faith in Christ. To the state the Lord has assigned the duty of keeping good order and peace, of punishing the wrongdoer, and of arranging all civil matters in society (Romans 13:3,4). The purpose is "that we may live peaceful and quiet lives in all godliness and holiness" (1 Timothy 2:2).

 In Old Testament Israel, the work of church and state were combined. Why do we speak of distinct responsibilities for church and state?

A: Israel was a unique nation in the world's history. God chose Israel as the nation from which he would bring the Savior. In addition, God intended that the gospel would spread from Israel to every other nation. "Although the whole earth is mine, you will be for me a kingdom of priests and a holy nation" (Exodus 19:5,6). No other nation in Old Testament times can be compared to Israel nor can any nation in New Testament times be compared to it. No nation today has been called by God to be his nation in any way similar to Israel. In fact, the visible Christian church today fits best as a comparison with the ancient nation of Israel. We must not draw principles concerning church and state today from the way God dealt with and governed Old Testament Israel. No nation today can claim to be God's special nation as Israel was.

It is much better to look at God's stated purposes for both church and state and to consider the tools he has given each. God has given a unique purpose to each and a unique tool for each to use to accomplish that purpose.

A careful look at Romans 13 will reveal that God has established the government for the physical protection of its citizens. The tool that God has given to the government to accomplish this task is the ability to enforce obedience by enacting laws and threatening punishment or penalties on the disobedient: "He is God's servant, an agent of wrath to bring punishment on the wrongdoer" (Romans 13:4).

How different are the task and tools entrusted to the church. The church is not concerned with outward behavior accomplished by threat and punishment. The purpose of the Christian church is to bring people to faith in Jesus and to help them grow and remain in faith so they can live their faith everyday. The church does not use threat and punishment to accomplish its task. Instead it uses the means of grace, that is, the gospel in Word and sacrament. Jesus tells us about the task and tools of the church in what is known as the Great Commission: "Go and make disciples of all nations, baptizing them in the name of the Father and of the Son and of the Holy Spirit, and teaching them to obey everything I have commanded you" (Matthew 28:19,20).

In summary, the church and the state have different goals. One is concerned with outward obedience, the other with inward faith. Church and state also have different tools. One uses laws and punishment to coerce obedience;

the other uses the gospel to win hearts for eternity and to change lives now. When either church or state meddles in the affairs of the other, damage is done to the purposes of both. The worst effect of all is the harm that is done to the true cause of the gospel.

3. We believe that the only means God has given to the church to carry out its assigned purpose are the Word and sacraments (Matthew 28:19,20). People are converted by the Holy Spirit only through the message of law and gospel, sin and grace, the wrath of God against sin and the mercy of God in Christ. We believe that the means given to the state to fulfill its assignment is civil law with its punishments and rewards, set up and used according to the light of reason (Romans 13:4). The light of reason includes the natural knowledge of God, the natural knowledge of the law, and conscience.

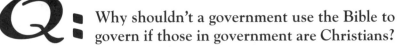 Why shouldn't a government use the Bible to govern if those in government are Christians?

A: Please read the previous question and answer first. In addition, we must realize that if a government uses the Bible to rule, then the government causes great confusion about the primary purpose for which the Bible was written. John sums up the main purpose of Holy Scripture when he summarizes his purpose for writing his gospel: "These are written that you may believe that Jesus is the Christ, the Son of God, and that by believing you may have life in his name" (John 20:31). When a government tries to rule by the Bible, it takes a book written primarily to bring hearts to faith and uses it to compel outward obedience through laws and punishments. The true purpose of the Bible—bringing people to faith—is pushed aside, and the Bible becomes a tool for getting people to do what the government wants them to do.

To state the problem simply: If a government begins to rule with the Bible, it would be trying to accomplish its God-given purpose—outward peace and earthly security—with a tool that is designed to accomplish a different purpose—inward peace and eternal security. Because the government would be using the Bible to coerce outward obedience, the message of the gospel would be easily distorted into a new law. That is why the work of the church is endangered whenever a government tries to use the Bible as its standard for ruling.

Rather than the Bible, God has given the governement the natural law inscribed in human hearts and the voice of conscience. Certainly human conscience can become clouded and confused in a sinful world. For that reason, the written moral law can help citizens understand more clearly that which is written on every heart. But a Christian will not begin to quote chapter and verse from the Bible as the basis for laws and morality. With an instructed conscience, he or she will appeal to other consciences and chart a course of action that will be just. Every conscience that has not been utterly hardened will recognize the truth of what the Christian is saying about morality. However, human sinfulness may not acknowledge the justice and truth of the natural law or the summary of it in the Bible.

Q: **Since God has commanded us not to murder, can the government execute a criminal?**

A: Just as God entrusts a bit of his authority to parents as they raise their children, so God has given a bit of his authority to governments as they seek to keep order and protect their citizens. While God forbids personal vengeance, the government is his tool to inflict justice on those who harm others. That is why God has entrusted to governments the power of "the sword" (Romans 13:4). The authority of "the sword" empowers governments to punish wrongdoers, even to the point of requiring their lives for violating the safety and security of others.

Q: Why doesn't our church take public stands on important social issues?

A: The church has been entrusted with just one mission in this world: to proclaim the gospel so that souls might be brought to faith and strengthened in faith. The improvement of society through a more just and honest social order is the task of government. God has not entrusted to his church the task of promoting a better social policy.

Yet individual Christians have two citizenships. Our most blessed "citizenship is in heaven" (Philippians 3:20), which Jesus has freely given to us by his life, death, and resurrection. But God has also blessed each of us with a role as a citizen of an earthly nation. Individual Christians or groups of Christians have a deep concern if our society and our government are guilty of injustice towards anyone. Christians have the privilege and obligation to work toward equal justice and social improvement. The church will work to encourage Christians to be the best citizens any country could have. As Christian citizens reflect the mercy of their merciful Father in heaven, they will look for ways to reflect his compassion and justice. Those efforts will also create opportunities to *witness to what is most important, the kingdom of heaven.*

4. We believe the proper relation is preserved between the church and the state only when each remains within its divinely assigned sphere and uses its divinely entrusted means. The church should not exercise civil authority nor interfere with the state as the state carries out its responsibilities. The state should not become a messenger of the gospel nor interfere with the church in its preaching mission. The church should not attempt to use the civil law and force to lead people to Christ. The state should not seek to govern by means of the gospel. On the other hand, the church and the state may cooperate in an endeavor as long as each remains within its assigned place and uses its entrusted means.

Q: Is it a greater danger if the church meddles in the affairs of the state or if the state meddles in the affairs of the church?

A: Both types of meddling can cause great harm to the work of the kingdom of God. Strong arguments can be made in both directions. When the government becomes involved in the work of the church, the real message of the gospel can be greatly hindered, even by well-meaning government officials.

Nevertheless, the greatest danger seems to exist when the church loses its focus on the work the Lord has given it and begins to meddle in the work God has given to the government. If the government meddles in the work of the church, at least the church can still remain focused on its mission of proclaiming the gospel. For example, the church prospered in the first centuries of its existence despite the many obstacles raised by the Roman Empire.

When the church meddles in the affairs of the state, the church has already begun to lose sight of its real calling from the Savior. Great damage to the cause of the gospel cannot help but happen at such times. For example, great problems developed once the Roman Empire became *officially* Christian. Very quickly the work of church and the work of state became confused. The real work of the gospel was often lost in the struggle for political power.

 Why should the state *not* govern by means of the gospel?

A: The gospel was not given by God for those who are agents of God's wrath "to bring punishment on the wrongdoer" (Romans 13:4). The gospel is a tool of the kingdom of God through which the Holy Spirit seeks to win hearts to trust in Christ for eternal life. The gospel was not given by God to coerce proper outward behavior from the citizens of an earthly country. Laws, based on conscience—threatening punishment on the disobedient and offering rewards for the obedient—are the proper tools of the state.

Q: Do church and state ever cooperate within the bounds of their God-given assignments?

A: Marriage is one example in which both church and state have an interest and in which they cooperate. The government wants good order to protect property and other legal rights. The government often demands a signed document, such as a marriage license. The church wants to make sure that Christian husbands and wives find God's rich blessings in their lifelong unions. The pastor serves as an agent of the state as he oversees the signing of the license and verifies it with his own signature. He serves in his role in Christ's kingdom as he instructs the couple in God's plan for marriage and speaks God's blessing on them as he unites them in God's gift of marriage.

The most frequent and important cooperation occurs when the church, through its public ministers, urges individual Christians to fulfill their roles as honest and responsible citizens of their country.

5. We believe that Christians are citizens of both realms and serve God by faithfully fulfilling their duties in both (Romans 13:6,7).

Q: How might Christians carry out their duties as citizens of an earthly nation?

A: Christians know the love of Jesus and seek always to live according to his will. They understand that Jesus desires them to live as law-abiding citizens in this world. In addition, Christians desire to show kindness, respect, and gentleness to others because they are disciples of Jesus.

Because Christians seek to love others, they will be good citizens in many specific ways. When they live where there is the freedom to vote, they will want to vote as well-informed citizens. In Christian love, they become informed about the issues and elect worthy candidates for public office. Where they see injustice, love motivates them to aid those suffering such injustice and to urge their representatives in government to correct the injustice.

They pray for all government officials and "all those in authority, that we may live peaceful and quiet lives in all godliness and holiness" (1 Timothy 2:2). They pay taxes. Christians may certainly use every legal deduction their government gives them, but they will also strive at the same time to be honest in reporting all income and in paying all taxes demanded by law. Christians do this in love for Christ so that their consciences do not risk bringing dishonor to the Savior's name. After all, as Paul reminds us, "This is also why you pay taxes, for the authorities are God's servants, who give their full time to governing. Give everyone what you owe him: If you owe taxes, pay taxes; if revenue, then revenue; if respect, then respect; if honor, then honor" (Romans 13:6,7).

Finally, wherever Christians enjoy religious freedom, they defend that freedom whenever it may be threatened. In all these ways, Christians support their government and conduct themselves as responsible citizens. Their real goal is to place no obstacle in the path of the gospel.

Q: **Since we are citizens of heaven first and foremost, why do we still need to obey the government under which we live?**

A: Simply, God has put us under the authority of two kingdoms in this world. We live under the gracious rule of the kingdom of Christ, and we also live under the rule of an earthly kingdom. Both have been ordained by Christ. Those who have authority over us in each kingdom are servants of Christ, even though unbelievers in government will not recognize their role as servants of Christ.

But the greatest reason to obey the earthly government is the spread of the gospel. The work of the gospel can thrive when a government functions well in protecting its citizens and their freedoms. Where there is anarchy and chaos because of weak or corrupt government, the work of the gospel is often hindered. Therefore, while it is true that our greatest and most real "citizenship is in heaven" (Philippians 3:20), our role and status as citizens of an earthly state are very significant as well.

Q: **Can Christians take oaths when they are required by the government?**

A: Some Christians have been bothered by the words of Christ in Matthew 5:34-37, which seem at first reading to prohibit any swearing in any situation by a Christian. Jesus said, "I tell you, Do not swear at all: either by heaven, for it is God's throne; or by the earth, for it is his footstool; or by Jerusalem, for it is the city of the Great King. And do not swear by your head, for you cannot make even one hair white or black. Simply let your 'Yes' be 'Yes,' and your 'No,' 'No'; anything beyond this comes from the evil one." However, it is clear from the context of this chapter (Jesus' Sermon on the Mount) and the rest of Scripture that his prohibition does not pertain to situations where an official and public witness of the truth is demanded of us for a testimony to others. For example, Jesus' command in Matthew 5 does not mean it is a sin to testify under oath in a court of law. Otherwise, Jesus himself would have sinned against his own prohibition when he allowed Caiaphas to put him under oath before the Sanhedrin (Matthew 26:63ff). Another example would be the public oaths taken by those elected or appointed to public office by which the other citizens know that the officials promise to carry out their tasks in accordance with the laws of the land.

What Jesus says in Matthew 5 does pertain to all our dealings in our private lives as we carry out our normal daily conversations with believers and unbelievers. There Jesus indeed absolutely prohibits us from calling on God—or anything else he has created—to witness to the truthfulness of our words. Jesus tells Christians to speak the truth simply and plainly and let it rest at that. When people learn that our words are honest, there is no need for additional embellishments to back up our statements.

Q: **What should a Christian do when he or she has suffered wrong and the wrongdoer is being punished by the civil government?**

A: "Do not take revenge, my friends, but leave room for God's wrath, for it is written: 'It is mine to avenge; I will repay,' says the Lord. On the contrary: 'If your enemy is hungry, feed him; if he is thirsty, give him something to drink. In doing this, you will heap burning coals on his head.' Do not be overcome by evil, but overcome evil with good" (Romans 12:19-21). With those words we are powerfully reminded that desires for vengeance and revenge are to be given no place in the hearts of those who live by the mercy of their Savior. While forgiving those who have caused us loss or pain is never easy, the power of Christ's free forgiveness and compassion for us causes us to find such compassion and forgiveness for others. That is the response God calls from us personally as citizens of heaven. In other words, if this matter were just between the one hurt and the one doing the hurting, the only action necessary would be to forgive.

Yet God makes punishing the wrongdoer the business of the government. The welfare of many others is also at stake. It is not by accident that Paul was inspired to write his words about government immediately after the warning about taking personal vengeance. If the government would allow those who have caused us loss or pain to go unpunished, the government would be encouraging the worst in sinful human nature to go unchecked and would be causing the hurt of many in society. Therefore, it is very important that we allow the justice system of our government to play its role as God's servant to "bring punishment on the wrongdoer" (13:4). That is one of the reasons God has given government to us as citizens of an earthly kingdom.

To put it all together, as Christians we rejoice in the blessing of a government through which God helps protect us, our families, and others in society. At the same time, we also guard against any lust for personal vengeance that our sinful nature harbors within. For example, it is not wrong for a Christian who has been the victim of a crime to testify in court to show the accused person the pain and suffering his or her loveless actions have caused. The government's justice that should follow may save many others from similar pain. But to speak angry and vengeful words or issue threats would reveal an unforgiving heart.

6. We reject any attempt by the state to restrict the free exercise of religion.

Q: Aren't we encouraging freedom for false teachers and false teachings by supporting the free exercise of religion?

A: By supporting the free exercise of religion, we are not supporting the false teachings of false prophets. Instead, we are merely acknowledging that God has not asked governments to decide what is false doctrine and what is true. Speaking spiritual truth and exposing false doctrine is not the work of the government but the church. In the public arena, we should work zealously to preserve freedom of religion, and in our calling as witnesses of Christ, we are to work even more zealously to proclaim the truth and unmask every deception of the devil. It is in our calling as royal priests of God that we seek to "demolish arguments and every pretension that sets itself up against the knowledge of God, and we take captive every thought to make it obedient to Christ" (2 Corinthians 10:5).

Q: What should we think about government-sponsored prayers at the openings of legislative sessions and other public functions?

A: As Psalm 50:15, "Call upon me in the day of trouble; I will deliver you, and you will honor me," reminds us, prayer is an act of worship on the part of believers by which we honor and glorify the only true God who hears and answers our prayers. Therefore, as with any act of outward worship, the principles of church fellowship apply (see the questions and answers under section VII on Church and Ministry).

Such public prayers are very often spoken in generic terms so as not to offend those who do not believe in Jesus as the eternal Son of God, the second person of the Trinity. Such prayers then become denials of the truth that Jesus is "the way and the truth and the life. No one comes to the Father except through [him]" (John 14:6). Prayers that do not approach the one true God through his eternal Son are nothing more than empty words spoken into the air that deceive unbelievers into thinking that they have been heard by God. Apart from Christ, these words of Isaiah 59:2 apply to our prayers, "Your iniquities have separated you from your God; your sins have hidden his face from you, so that he will not hear."

Another problem with such prayers is a confusion of the work of church and the work of state. Individual Christians, and Christian congregations, will certainly offer up prayers daily for their government. However, to do so publicly as part of the work of government is to mix the earthly kingdom with the kingdom of God.

Q: Do we believe in a strict separation of church and state?

A: Except for a few places where the work of these two kingdoms intersects (such as marriage) and except for the fact that individual Christians play a role in both kingdoms, we do believe in the separation of church and state. God has given different goals to these two institutions. He has established both. The government works for outward social peace. The church works to establish inward peace of conscience through the forgiveness of sins. In addition, God has given these two institutions different tools. The state uses laws with threats and penalties to force outward compliance. The church, while also calling sinners to repentance with God's revealed law, uses the gospel to work a change in human hearts. Any mixture of church and state damages the purposes and blessings that God intended to give us separately through each institution.

7. We reject any views that look to the church to guide and influence the state directly in the conduct of its affairs.

Q: What would be some examples of the church stepping out of its role by giving direct guidance to the state in its affairs?

A: If the church would ask the government to punish false teaching, it would be at work to coerce consciences by the threat of outward laws. If the Christian church would ask the government for special favors of legislation not granted to other religions in that country, it would be trying to gain acceptance by something other than the gospel. If a church body would try to influence legislation that does not directly affect the freedom of religion, it would have forgotten that Christ's gospel, not earthly laws, accomplishes the work of his kingdom. At the same time, individual Christians should voice their opinions about governmental action and even join organizations to work for candidates and legislations that they deem important.

Q: Why does our synod refrain from participating in the military chaplaincy to the armed forces?

A: It is not the government's responsibility to provide for the spiritual needs of its citizens. Our synod should be willing to bear the expense of sending out our own civilian chaplains to serve the spiritual needs of our members serving in the military. We send such chaplains to serve military forces stationed in foreign countries. The government has the responsibility to allow our civilian chaplains access to the military personnel in need of our spiritual ministry.

In the military chaplaincy currently practiced, the government insists that its military chaplains offer spiritual services to members of many different denominations. The government recognizes no difference in the various Protestant faiths and expects chaplains to carry out a generic Protestant ministry to all such members of the military. Such least-common-denominator religious services are impossible for anyone striving to proclaim all the truth of Scripture. That is why the questions of fellowship dealt with under section VII (Church and Ministry) also come into play here.

8. We reject any attempt on the part of the church to seek the financial assistance of the state in carrying out its saving purpose.

Q: Since God's Old Testament people received help from the Persian king to complete the rebuilding of the temple, doesn't that set an example for what would be proper today?

A: First of all, there is a difference between what Scripture merely describes as happening and what it commands for us to believe or do. The first are called descriptive passages of Scripture, and they do not necessarily set up an example for us to follow. The second are called prescriptive passages, and those passages direct our thoughts, words, and actions. The help of the Persian kings in the rebuilding of the temple in Jerusalem as it is described in the book of Ezra clearly fits best under the descriptive passages of Scripture. It is not a command for us to follow. It is simply a description of what happened as the temple was rebuilt.

With that said, some of the help given by Persia was nothing more than restoring to the temple the riches that had been stolen by the Babylonian King Nebuchadnezzar when he had plundered Jerusalem. Other help appears to have been given without any specific requests on the part of God's people. To accept gifts freely offered from those outside the church—even the government—is not forbidden in Scripture. Yet it would be a clear confusion of the two kingdoms in which we actively live if Christians sought direct support for the work of the gospel from the government.

9. We reject any views that hold that citizens are free to disobey such laws of the state with which they disagree on the basis of personal judgment.

 What would be some examples of Christians disobeying a law of the government with which they simply had a personal disagreement?

A: If Christians tried to excuse themselves from paying taxes because they believed their government was wasting their money, that would simply be a personal disagreement used as an excuse to disobey the government. Another example might be a Christian refusing to serve in the armed forces when his or her country is in the midst of a just war on the part of the government. A third example might be a Christian who disagrees with the state's seatbelt laws and purposefully flaunts his or her lack of compliance.

Q: Why would it be wrong in these cases to apply the principle that we are to obey God rather than man?

A: When Peter and the other apostles told the Jewish Sanhedrin, "We must obey God rather than men!" (Acts 5:29), they were responding to a demand from their government to stop sharing the gospel, which Jesus had commanded them to do. We only have the right to disobey our government if our government explicitly forbids us to do what God commands or if it requires us to do what God forbids. In the examples in the previous question, the government is not forcing us into situations where we would be sinning by following its laws.

Even in cases where our government's laws or regulations may be foolish, those who serve in our government still remain servants of God (Romans 13:6) and deserve honor and obedience. Of course, in a free country, we certainly can exercise our ability to let our views be known at the ballot box or in personal correspondence with our representatives.

Additional Reading for This Section:

Civil Government: God's Other Kingdom by Daniel M. Deutschlander
Church—Mission—Ministry: The Family of God by Armin W. Schuetze
Stewardship: What I Do with What God Gave Me by Arno J. Wolfgramm

Section IX.
JESUS' RETURN AND THE JUDGMENT

> 1. We believe that Jesus, true God and true man, who rose from death and ascended to the right hand of the Father, will come again. He will return visibly, in the same way as his disciples saw him go into heaven (Acts 1:11).

Q: **Since Jesus is already with us until the end of all time, how can we speak of him as returning?**

A: Jesus reminds us in Matthew 28:20, "Surely I am with you always." He is present with us as both God and man every moment of every day. However, at the present time he is not visible. On the Last Day, he will once again reveal his presence in the clouds of heaven just as he did when he left his disciples on the Day of Ascension. The Scripture reminds us, "Look, he is coming with the clouds, and every eye will see him" (Revelation 1:7). Because he will once again reveal his visible form, we speak of Jesus' returning. It is also interesting to note that one of the common words used in the Greek New Testament for Jesus' second coming has the basic meaning of "appearing."

Q: **What will be different from his first coming?**

A: The same Jesus who is fully God and fully man and was born of the virgin Mary will appear on the Last Day. Yet after that the similarities cease. At his first coming, Jesus chose to humble himself by not always or not fully using his divine power and glory. He did this willingly out of love for us so that he could suffer and die for us all. When Jesus describes his second coming, he pictures it like this: "When the Son of Man comes in his glory, and all the angels with him, he will sit on his throne in heavenly glory" (Matthew 25:31). At his first coming, as a humble baby in a manger, most could have easily ignored who he truly was. That will not be the case at his return. On the Last Day, all will instantly know that the One appearing in great power and glory is Jesus of Nazareth. While in his first appearance he came as the Suffering Servant of all, at his second coming he will be the glorious judge of the living and the dead.

Q: **Didn't Jesus stop being true man at his ascension? How can we say then that the one returning is still both true God and true man?**

A: It is a common misconception to think that Jesus ceased being a true human being after his ascension. But listen to the words of the angels on the day of his ascension: "This same Jesus, who has been taken from you into heaven, will come back in the same way you have seen him go into heaven" (Acts 1:11). It was Jesus, both God and man, whose visible presence was removed from the earth on the hill of ascension. It is that same Jesus, still God and man, who will return in the clouds of heaven on the Last Day. The apostle Paul wrote about Jesus to Timothy several decades after the ascension of Jesus: "For there is one God and one mediator between God and men, the man Christ Jesus" (1 Timothy 2:5).

Christians find practical importance in remembering that Jesus is still both God and man. When believers approach Jesus in prayer, they come not only to a powerful God who can help in every need, but they also come to their brother who is still flesh and blood as they are. The author to the Hebrews picked up on that beautiful truth when he wrote, "For we do not have a high priest who is unable to sympathize with our weaknesses, but we have one who has been tempted in every way, just as we are—yet was without sin" (4:15).

2. We believe that no one can know the exact time of Jesus' return. This knowledge is hidden even from the angels in heaven (Matthew 24:36). Nevertheless, our Lord has given signs to his believers to keep them in constant expectation of his return (Matthew 24:4-14). He has told them to be alert and to watch so that day will not come upon them unexpectedly (Luke 21:34).

 Jesus says that even he does not know the time of the end of the world (Matthew 24:36). How can he not know the time of the end when he is the all-knowing God?

A: It is very important to notice when Jesus spoke those words of Matthew 24:36. It was during the time when Jesus had humbled himself in order to suffer and die as our substitute. We call that period, from his conception in the womb of his mother to his death and burial, his state of humiliation. It is most fully described for us in Philippians 2:6-8. During that period, Jesus did not always make full or complete use of the divine power and glory he possessed. In other words, although as true God Jesus was and always remained omniscient, according to his human nature, at the very same time he did not always choose to make use of that knowledge.

Of course, exactly how Jesus could know all things and yet not know all things goes beyond our limited ability to grasp and understand. It is the same question that arises when we think about God being eternal and yet the God-man Jesus dying. Paul's words describe his wonder as he contemplated the incarnation: "Beyond all question, the mystery of godliness is great" (1 Timothy 3:16).

Q: Why have so many tried to predict the exact date of Jesus' return?

A: Proud and stubborn sinful human nature is always vainly trying to uncover what God has kept hidden. Think of the popularity of psychics and others who claim to predict the future. Even though Scripture repeatedly speaks of Jesus' return coming suddenly, "like a thief in the night" (1 Thessalonians 5:2), human beings are fascinated by predicting future events. All they accomplish is making themselves look foolish with their predictions. Their false predictions of the future give an unbelieving world another reason to believe that it can scoff at any idea of being called into judgment by God.

Q: Why does God hide the exact time of the Last Day?

A: God has hidden all the details of the future from us, including his timetable for the Last Day. Just before Jesus ascended, the disciples wanted to know if it was time for Jesus to usher in the last events of the world's history. They asked, "'Lord, are you at this time going to restore the kingdom to Israel?' He said to them: 'It is not for you to know the times or dates the Father has set by his own authority. But you will receive power when the Holy Spirit comes on you; and you will be my witnesses'" (Acts 1:6-8). Our lives would be dramatically different if we knew the future, not necessarily different in a good sense. We would dread the coming of catastrophes, mourn the losses of loved ones beforehand, and even lose moments of joy and happiness that could not surprise us. God considered it enough for us to know that he would care for us and that Jesus would return.

Perhaps if people knew when the Lord would return, they would spend their lives pursuing pleasure and wealth rather than seeking God and his grace in Jesus. They would postpone serious consideration of God's message. Perhaps even Christians would more easily be tempted to think about spiritual matters only at the last possible moment—the eleventh hour. Such carelessness may kill our faith by giving reign to our sinful nature. We would set aside the Savior's encouragement to be salt and light in this world (Matthew 5:13-16). Yet if we would know when the Last Day is coming but would not know when our deaths would occur, we would gain nothing. Death ends the human journey on earth as suddenly as the coming of the Last Day.

In his wisdom, God withheld the knowledge of the future from us and urged us to be ready at all times. He gives us each day to enjoy the blessings and the opportunities of each day. Each day is a time given to us by God to serve him, love others, and enjoy all his blessings. Believers have the special responsibility of sharing the gospel with others while they have opportunity. Jesus encourages us, "As long as it is day, we must do the work of him who sent me. Night is coming, when no one can work" (John 9:4).

Q: What does Jesus mean when he urges us to be alert and to watch for his return?

A: Paul sums up what it means to be spiritually alert and watching in 1 Thessalonians 5:4-11: "But you, brothers, are not in darkness so that this day should surprise you like a thief. You are all sons of the light and sons of the day. We do not belong to the night or to the darkness. So then, let us not be like others, who are asleep, but let us be alert and self-controlled. For those who sleep, sleep at night, and those who get drunk, get drunk at night. But since we belong to the day, let us be self-controlled, putting on faith and love as a breast-plate, and the hope of salvation as a helmet. For God did not appoint us to suffer wrath but to receive salvation through our Lord Jesus Christ. He died for us so that, whether we are awake or asleep, we may live together with him. Therefore encourage one another and build each other up, just as in fact you are doing." To be alert and awake means to be "self-controlled" by daily refusing to let our old sinful nature rule us with its sins and desires. Instead, every day we put "on faith and love as a breastplate, and the hope of salvation as a helmet." As we turn from sin to our Savior, we live in joyful faith that salvation is ours and that we have nothing to fear when Jesus returns. We can, therefore, also use every opportunity to practice our love for God and others until our lives end or Christ returns. In his Small Catechism, Luther called such alert and watchful living a daily return to the grace and power of our baptism.

 Since many of the signs of the end of which Jesus spoke have been around for centuries, how can he say that such events are signs of his return?

A: Indeed, many of the signs Jesus mentions are nothing new. Wars, rumors of war, famines, and earthquakes have been around as long as humans can remember. Yet every one of those signs, and others like them, is a reminder that the world as we know it is falling apart because of human sin and God's curse on the fallen world. Paul spoke of the decay of this present world under God's curse in Romans 8:20,21: "For the creation was subjected to frustration, not by its own choice, but by the will of the one who subjected it, in hope that the creation itself will be liberated from its bondage to decay and brought into the glorious freedom of the children of God." Every time we see the physical world, or the inhabitants of this world, struggling because of what sin has done to an otherwise perfect creation, we are reminded of the hope of the new heaven and the new earth that will begin when our Lord returns.

 Since he promised that he was coming soon, for 20 centuries Christians have eagerly waited for Jesus' return. Why has Jesus urged his believers to be ready when he has so long delayed his return?

A: Peter simply answers this question: "But do not forget this one thing, dear friends: With the Lord a day is like a thousand years, and a thousand years are like a day. The Lord is not slow in keeping his promise, as some understand slowness. He is patient with you, not wanting anyone to perish, but everyone to come to repentance" (2 Peter 3:8,9). Peter makes two important points. First, he reminds us that our concept of "slowness" is only from our vantage point. From God's perspective, we might say that it has been only two days since Jesus' death, resurrection, and ascension. Second, any apparent delay is not carelessness on God's part. His apparent delay serves only one purpose: the patient extension of this world's time of grace so that the gospel might continue to rescue sinners from eternal judgment.

Consider also that no Christian has ever been harmed by being ready for the Last Day. It is a misconception that it would be much better to be able to live carelessly in sin rather than carefully in faith, hope, and love in Christ. Living in faith in Christ and in love for him and others causes us to lose nothing that is really valuable in life. In fact, as Jesus assures us, only those who know and believe in him "have life, and have it to the full" (John 10:10).

Q: Do we really live in the last days?

A: There are two ways to answer this question. In the broadest terms and in accord with the most common biblical usage of the phrase "last days," we can indeed be sure that we live in those last days. The last days were ushered in by Jesus' first appearing and will end with his second appearing on the Last Day. That is made clear by Peter on Pentecost when he quoted from the prophet Joel to describe what was happening already on the first Pentecost day: "This is what was spoken by the prophet Joel: 'In the last days, God says, I will pour out my Spirit on all people'" (Acts 2:16,17). Clearly, if Peter lived during the last days, we certainly live in them as well.

To some, the words *last days* may have a narrower definition. They may mean the very last years, months, or days before Jesus' return. That detail God has chosen in loving wisdom to hide from our view. We can never know for sure if we live in those very last years, months, or days before his return. As Christians, we live so that we are ready if Jesus would return in the next moment.

3. We believe that at Jesus' return this present world will come to an end. "In keeping with his promise we are looking forward to a new heaven and a new earth, the home of righteousness" (2 Peter 3:13).

Q : Will Jesus come only once more at the end of the world?

A : Jesus came once to accomplish our salvation and will come again at the end of time. The author to the Hebrews makes it clear that there are only two visible comings of Christ in the history of this world: "Just as man is destined to die once, and after that to face judgment, so Christ was sacrificed once to take away the sins of many people; and he will appear a second time, not to bear sin, but to bring salvation to those who are waiting for him" (9:27,28). Many other passages in Scripture identify this second appearance of Christ with the very last day of this world's existence, not at some point earlier than that. When Jesus returns on that day, he will bring the full joy of heaven to those who believe. Christ's return, the resurrection of both believer and unbeliever, the final judgment of all unbelievers, and the beginning of the full enjoyment of heaven for every believer will all take place on the day of Jesus' second coming. Jesus himself reminds us of that truth: "For my Father's will is that everyone who looks to the Son and believes in him shall have eternal life, and I will raise him up at the last day" (John 6:40). To speak of any third or fourth coming of Christ to this world is to go beyond Scripture.

Q : What does Scripture mean when it speaks of a new heaven and a new earth?

A : The new heaven (or heavens) and the new earth are spoken of in Isaiah, 2 Peter, and Revelation. These are other names for the place where believers will enjoy the visible presence of God in perfection forever. The names "new heaven" and "new earth" are most often used for the dwelling of believers after the Last Day when the present creation will cease to exist and a new one—never to be marred by sin—will take its place.

 Some, like the Jehovah's Witnesses, teach that the present world will never be destroyed. How do they try to support such a teaching from Scripture?

They can't! The wording of this current creation's final fate is simply too clear to misunderstand. The description of the destruction of the current universe can't be put any more simply than how Peter relates it in his second epistle when he writes, "But the day of the Lord will come like a thief. The heavens will disappear with a roar; the elements will be destroyed by fire, and the earth and everything in it will be laid bare" (2 Peter 3:10).

4. We believe that when Jesus returns and his voice is heard throughout the earth, all the dead will rise, that is, their souls will be reunited with their bodies (John 5:28,29). Together with those still living, the resurrected will appear before his throne of judgment. The unbelievers will be condemned to an eternity in hell. Those who by faith have been cleansed in the blood of Christ will be glorified and will live with Jesus forever in the blessed presence of God in heaven (Philippians 3:21).

How can Jesus return in such a way that he is visibly and audibly present to everyone in the whole world at the same instant?

A: We must remember that "nothing is impossible with God" (Luke 1:37). God tells us that the world as we know it will cease to exist, and at that very same moment, all will see Christ as he returns. Scripture tells us, "Look, he is coming with the clouds, and every eye will see him, even those who pierced him" (Revelation 1:7). It is not just those who are alive when the Last Day arrives who will instantly see Christ. All who have ever lived, having been raised back to life in "the twinkling of an eye" (1 Corinthians 15:52), will also be present to see him.

Q: How will God raise all the dead when many who died long ago have returned to dust?

A: He who once "formed the man from the dust of the ground and breathed into his nostrils the breath of life" (Genesis 2:7) will not have any trouble reassembling dust into human beings. After all, our God can "do immeasurably more than all we ask or imagine" (Ephesians 3:20).

Q: What does Scripture mean when it tells us that God will give believers glorified bodies after the resurrection?

A: Human beings changed after the fall into sin. The body that had been immortal became mortal. A world that knew no bodily weaknesses, imperfections, or illnesses became all too familiar with them. Human bodies that would have known no process of aging and decay suddenly were subject to just that.

All of that will change again on the Last Day. The apostle Paul makes just such comparisons in 1 Corinthians 15 where he writes, "The body that is sown [buried] is perishable, it is raised imperishable; it is sown in dishonor, it is raised in glory; it is sown in weakness, it is raised in power; it is sown a natural body, it is raised a spiritual body" (1 Corinthians 15:42-44). All that sin has done to our bodies in this sinful world will be reversed. Our bodies will never again be subject to illnesses, weaknesses, disabilities, or death. And one more thing! "The Lord Jesus Christ . . . will transform our lowly bodies so that they will be like his glorious body" (Philippians 3:20,21). It appears that we will have an outward glory like the glorious body of our risen Lord. We will have to wait until heaven to understand exactly what that will be like!

Q: **Since the souls of those who died before the Last Day have already gone to heaven or hell, what is the purpose of having all stand before God on judgment day?**

A: Think of how often in this world God's perfect justice and righteousness is called into question—even, all too often, by believers! On the Last Day, God will assemble all who have ever lived and reveal the absolute perfection and justice of all his judgments. In the presence of all nations, he will give clear evidence from the lives of all unbelievers that they truly earned the judgment so many had already begun to receive since they died before the Last Day. He will also proclaim with more irrefutable evidence from the lives of his believers that they put their trust in Jesus and received eternal life as a free and gracious inheritance. On the Last Day, God will not frantically try to figure out what he is going to do with all these people. Rather, the Last Day establishes the perfect justice of the eternal fate of all those who gather before him. For the simplest evidence of this, refer to Matthew 25:31ff.

Q: **How can a loving God condemn people, body and soul, to eternal hell?**

A: God is both perfect love and perfect justice. He cannot cease being either love or justice and still remain God. In perfect, unconditional love through Jesus, God provides full forgiveness for all sinners who have ever lived. In amazing patience he offers that forgiveness through the gospel again and again to a world that hates him by nature. Only when humanity persists in stubborn unbelief and hatred of God does God condemn people, body and soul, to eternal hell. Is it really his perfect justice that is most astounding to understand or his love that would kill his own beloved Son so that the enemies who hate him might live with him forever?

Q: **Will we still have the same relationships in heaven with those whom we know in this life?**

A: There are two sides to the answer to this question. First, consider Jesus' answer to the Sadducees in Matthew 22:23ff. The Sadducees neither believed in the eternity of the soul nor in the resurrection of the body. They tried to ridicule any idea of eternal life by raising the question of a woman who was married to seven husbands, all who preceded her in death. Whose wife will she be? they wondered. As part of his reply to their question, Jesus said, "At the resurrection people will neither marry nor be given in marriage; they will be like the angels in heaven" (Matthew 22:30). From those words it seems best to say that marriage and family life as we know it in this life will not continue. While that may sadden us, remember that one of the reasons we rejoice in family in this sinful world is that family surrounds us with people who care deeply about us in an uncaring world. In heaven the family of God functions in perfect love for every family member. We don't really suffer a loss at all but a gain as we enjoy the perfect companionship of the full family of God. In other words, our concept of a joyful reunion in heaven is not too large. It is too small when we think of it only as the reunion of husband and wife or the reunion of dear friends we have known here. We will be reunited with all believers who will have perfect and full love for us in heaven!

But there is another side to this question. Even though marriage and family life as we know them cease in eternity, that does not mean that we suddenly lose our identity or our significance to others. For instance, consider Jesus' transfiguration when Moses and Elijah appeared with him on the mountain. Although they were living in heaven, they had not ceased being Moses and Elijah. They had not lost their identities or life histories when they entered heaven. So too it appears that we will remain who we are—and so will those we have known.

Part of the problem we are struggling with here is the fact that heaven is so wondrous that we have no concrete experience or words from this life to fully describe it. Paul had that difficulty after he was given a vision of the glory of heaven: "He heard inexpressible things, things that man is not permitted [which could also be translated: "things that it is not possible . . ."] to tell" (2 Corinthians 12:4). Rest assured, not one of us will be disappointed nor will we ask for a refund of the price Christ paid to win heaven for us!

Q: **What will it be like to live in God's presence?**

A: John the apostle spoke of one of the greatest joys of heaven: "When he appears, we shall be like him, for we shall see him as he is" (1 John 3:2). This vision of God will be our delight for all eternity. Christians cannot even remotely comprehend the joy of actually being able to see God and to exist forever in the visible glory of his presence. Is it any wonder that the saints and angels pictured before the throne of God in heaven are often found falling to the ground in astonishment and wonder? See, for example, Revelation 19:1ff.

Scripture gives us other details of the wonders awaiting us in the presence of our gracious and glorious God: "They are before the throne of God and serve him day and night in his temple; and he who sits on the throne will spread his tent over them. Never again will they hunger; never again will they thirst. The sun will not beat upon them, nor any scorching heat. For the Lamb at the center of the throne will be their shepherd; he will lead them to springs of living water. And God will wipe away every tear from their eyes" (Revelation 7:15-17). All the troubles that sin has brought into our lives will be absent in heaven.

Notice even in this passage that often the best Scripture can do for us is simply to list what won't be in heaven (sin and all its evil effects). The true glory and wonder of what it will be like to live in God's presence will only be known when by the grace of Jesus we experience them firsthand.

5. We reject the teaching that Christ will reign on earth for a thousand years in a physical, earthly kingdom. This teaching (millennialism) has no valid scriptural basis and falsely leads Christians to set their hopes upon an earthly kingdom of Christ (John 18:36). We reject as unscriptural any claim that Christians will be physically removed, or "raptured," from the earth prior to judgment day. We likewise reject as unscriptural any claim that all the Jews will be converted in the final days.

Q: **What is millennialism?**

A: Millennialism is the false teaching that Christians will enjoy a glorious visible kingdom on earth for one thousand years before the final judgment. *Millennium* means "one thousand years." Some teach that the second coming of Jesus will not take place until after the millennium is over. They are called *post*-millennialists. Others teach that the second coming of Jesus will take place before the millennium. They are called *pre*-millennialists.

Q: If Revelation 20 does not teach millennialism, what does it mean?

A: Just as in mathematics you don't use the more difficult forms (such as calculus or trigonometry) to reexplain or teach the basics (addition and subtraction), so also in biblical interpretation it is a dangerous thing to use the more difficult passages to reexplain or reinterpret the more basic passages. The reason for rejecting the false ideas of a glorious earthly millennium is that the Bible does not mention any such visible, glorious earthly reign of Christians on earth in the most basic sections speaking about the end of the world. Instead, Scripture speaks of a great falling away from the faith. It speaks of love growing cold as history draws to its conclusion (Matthew 24:9ff). Far from leading us to hope for better days for this world, Scripture repeatedly urges us to set our sights on heaven and eternity. "Since, then, you have been raised with Christ, set your hearts on things above, where Christ is seated at the right hand of God. Set your minds on things above, not on earthly things. For you died, and your life is now hidden with Christ in God. When Christ, who is your life, appears, then you also will appear with him in glory" (Colossians 3:1-4).

In addition, millennialists ignore significant points of interpretation in Revelation 20, which they claim teaches this supposed earthly period of a one-thousand-year rule of Christians on earth. They ignore that much of Revelation 20 is clearly figurative, describing realities in terminology that is not meant to be taken literally. For example, millennialists insist that we take the "thousand years" of verses 2 and 4 literally, yet in the midst of this vision they do not insist that the "chain" that binds Satan in verse 1 be taken literally. While seeing one figure of speech, they refuse to see the other—the "thousand years"—right next to it.

In addition, verse 4 says, "I saw thrones on which were seated those who had been given authority to judge." Millennialists fail to note that whenever "thrones" are mentioned in Revelation, the thrones are in heaven and not on earth. Why would that be different here? Verse 4 identifies those who are ruling on these thrones not as living believers visibly ruling the world but as the "souls of those who had been beheaded because of their testimony for Jesus and because of the word of God."

Simply, a literal reading of Revelation 20 that makes it fit the idea of an earthly, glorious, visible rule of Christians on earth is a careless rendering and leads to a distortion of other simpler and clearer sections of Scripture.

Q: **What do some Christians mean when they speak about the rapture?**

A: Some Christians believe that Jesus will secretly return sometime before judgment day to take all his believers from this world so that they can be with him in heaven and not struggle anymore on earth. They tell us that life in the world will go on, but suddenly all the believers will be *missing*. Many who teach the rapture believe that this will occur before the seven years of the great tribulation that comes immediately before what they call the millennium. These people are called *pre-tribulationists*. Others teach that this rapture occurs in the middle of those years of tribulation; these people are called *mid-tribulationists*. Still others teach that the rapture occurs at the end of the seven years of tribulation, immediately before the beginning of the millennium. These people are called *post-tribulationists*.

Q: ■ Doesn't 1 Thessalonians 4:16,17 teach a rapture of believers before the Last Day?

A: Those who believe that 1 Thessalonians 4:16,17 teaches a rapture of believers before the Last Day do not pay attention to the context of that passage. Paul was addressing the Thessalonian Christians concerning a misunderstanding they had about those who died in the faith. They were expecting Christ to return so intently that they were afraid that Christians among them who died before Christ's return might be lost. This was leading to hopeless despair on the part of the Christians who mourned those who died.

Paul, therefore, was comforting them with the assurance that far from being lost, those dead Christians would rise to meet Christ in the air on the Last Day. Those dead Christians wouldn't be left behind; in fact, they would be "first" in being gathered to Christ—first when compared to the living believers! "First" *they* will be raised from the dead, rejoined body and soul, and caught up in the clouds to meet Jesus, "then" the believers still living will be gathered to meet Jesus with them. If we want to use the term *rapture*, it would be this gathering of all believers, living and dead, with Jesus in the clouds of heaven on judgment day.

In other words, this passage says nothing about unbelievers. They are not in the context of the discussion at all in 1 Thessalonians 4. To say that this passage teaches that believers will be raised first and then a thousand years later the dead unbelievers will be raised inserts something into the context that is not in Paul's words. For further proof, notice the passages of Scripture that clearly have believers and unbelievers rising on the very same day, the Last Day: Daniel 12:2; John 5:28,29; and John 6:40.

Q: **Why are the false teachings of millennialism and the rapture so dangerous to Christian faith?**

A: The rapture gives false hope that God will remove his Christians from this earth before things get too bad, and the millennium emphasizes a wonderful golden age for the gospel in this world. Both work against the biblical emphasis that "we must go through many hardships to enter the kingdom of God" (Acts 14:22). How easy it would be for a Christian who buys into these deceptions to be surprised and unprepared for how difficult it actually is for the Christian to live in a hostile world this side of heaven. Scripture does not promise, "Don't worry; the rapture or the millennium is coming so it will never get too bad for you." Instead, Scripture prepares us to face severe difficulties and trials in this life. At the same time, the Bible draws our attention to the glory that will be ours in eternity: "I consider that our present sufferings are not worth comparing with the glory that will be revealed in us" (Romans 8:18).

In addition, the millennium distorts what Christ's kingdom is all about. The kingdom of God is established within the hearts of people by the power of the Holy Spirit working through the gospel in Word and sacrament. God's kingdom is not something visible or external this side of heaven. Christ's kingdom is not about earthly power or setting up an impressive governmental system. As Jesus himself said to Pilate, "My kingdom is not of this world" (John 18:36). Millennialism fans see false hopes of outward glory for Christ's kingdom and his people in this world. Such hopes will prove empty. What is even more dangerous is that those false hopes and dreams take the Christian's attention away from the crucial matters of the heart—daily repentance and trust in forgiveness. "The kingdom of God is not a matter of eating and drinking, but of righteousness, peace and joy in the Holy Spirit" (Romans 14:17).

Both the rapture and the teaching of the millennium teach a second chance for those who are not prepared the first time Jesus returns to rescue his own. This works against the urgency Scripture speaks about, both for our being ready for Jesus' return and for making the most of every opportunity now to help others be ready when he returns.

Q: Paul wrote that "all Israel will be saved" (Romans 11:26). Will all Jews be converted in the final days?

A: This is a common misunderstanding that doesn't recognize that in the New Testament, "Israel" refers to those who have Abraham's faith, not those who have Abraham's blood in their veins. "You are all sons of God through faith in Christ Jesus, for all of you who were baptized into Christ have clothed yourselves with Christ. There is neither Jew nor Greek, slave nor free, male nor female, for you are all one in Christ Jesus. If you belong to Christ, then you are Abraham's seed, and heirs according to the promise" (Galatians 3:26-29). While those physically descended from Abraham were the outward nation of Israel those who believe in the promised Savior—whether they have the blood of Abraham in their veins or not are the true spiritual Israel. Even in the Old Testament, Ruth, Rahab, and others were not children of Abraham by blood. Notice how Paul emphasizes that the true Israelites are those who "belong to Christ."

Also in Romans 9, Paul is not teaching that all those who have the blood of Abraham in their veins are going to be found in heaven simply because of their genes. By "all Israel" he is speaking of the total number of both Jews and Gentiles who will be converted. He is referring to the true spiritual *Israel*. A few verses earlier in the same chapter of Romans, Paul clearly stated that "not all who are descended from Israel are Israel" (Romans 9:6). It is the clear and consistent message of Scripture that only those who are brought to repentance and faith in Jesus Christ will be found in heaven. Nowhere does God promise that the people of an entire nation will be brought to faith simply because of their bloodline.

6. We reject the teaching that Christians should look for one individual to arise in the end times as the great Antichrist. The characteristics of the Antichrist as presented in Scripture have been and are being fulfilled in the institution of the papacy (2 Thessalonians 2:4-10). We reject the opinion that the identification of the papacy with the Antichrist was merely a historical judgment valid only at the time of the Reformation.

Q: What does Scripture mean with the term *antichrist*?

A: The Greek equivalent of our English prefix "anti" has a dual meaning. Its most basic meaning is "in the place of," that is, someone or something serving as a substitute. However, since someone who is "in the place of" someone else can actually work against the one whose place he or she takes, the meaning can also simply be "against." The basic idea of *antichrist* in Scripture uses both ideas. The Antichrist is someone who stands in the place of Christ within his church but actually works against Christ and as an enemy of the truth of Christ's gospel.

Q : Does Scripture speak of one Antichrist or many antichrists?

A : Scripture speaks of both. Scripture warns of many *antichrists*. Then the term is similar to the term *false prophets*. All false prophets work to turn people's hearts away from Christ. But Scripture also warns us about one great Antichrist who, more than anyone, will cause confusion and havoc in the kingdom of God. As 2 Thessalonians 2:4 tells us, he will cause this confusion by setting "himself up in God's temple" while serving in reality as an ally of Satan. In other words, he will be within the visible Christian church, as an enemy of the truth. The apostle John mentions both "antichrists" and the "antichrist" in his first epistle: "Dear children, this is the last hour; and as you have heard that the antichrist is coming, even now many antichrists have come" (1 John 2:18).

Q : Since Scripture does not specifically tell us that the papacy is the great Antichrist, aren't we going beyond Scripture to teach this as divinely revealed doctrine?

A : God intended Old Testament messianic prophecies to help believers at the time of Christ identify the true Messiah, even though not a single prophecy ever said, "His name is Jesus, and his mother's name is Mary!" From these Old Testament descriptions of the Messiah, God intended his people to be able to draw conclusions about the specific identity of the Savior when he appeared.

In much the same way, the New Testament provides believers with specific descriptions of the person and work of the great

Antichrist so that we could recognize him when he appeared on the scene. If Scripture never intended us to use its descriptions of the great Antichrist to identify him when he appeared, why would God have given us so much detail to use? Just look at all the details revealed about the great Antichrist in 2 Thessalonians 2. The whole purpose of identifying his characteristics and work is so that Christians could recognize him and avoid his lies and deceits. The Antichrist will fool many and lead many to spiritual destruction. To refuse to draw the conclusion that the papacy is the great Antichrist is to endanger souls by failing to give a warning about his deadly false doctrines.

Q: **Isn't our doctrine of the Antichrist only a reflection of historical animosity between Catholics and Lutherans?**

A: Certainly there have been times in the course of history when disagreements between Catholics and Lutherans have flared up, even into military conflict. At times the disagreements have been more hostile partisan politics than those of conscientious biblical disagreement. But the Lutheran doctrine of the Antichrist is not such partisan politics. In fact, in the centuries of church history, there have been voices within the Catholic church itself who have drawn the same conclusion about the papacy. That should not surprise us, since this doctrine rests on clear scriptural testimony. A detailed study of 2 Thessalonians 2:1-12 reveals so many details of the Antichrist's identity that it would be spiritual deception *not* to point to the papacy as being the very Antichrist of Scripture.

Q: **By declaring the papacy to be the Antichrist, what are we saying about the many millions who belong to the church body that the papacy leads?**

A: It is a grave spiritual danger to belong to a church whose official head teaches that salvation is not by Christ alone but also by human cooperation. It is harmful to souls to belong to a church that teaches that Jesus is not our only mediator between the Father and us and that offers Mary as a needed "friend of Christians." Such examples of false doctrines within the Roman Catholic Church could continue for many pages. To believe and accept as truth all that the Roman Catholic Church officially teaches is incompatible with the biblical concept of saving faith.

Yet the power of the gospel persists. Because traces of the gospel truth are included in its liturgy and hymns and because many Roman Catholics read their Bible, where the truth of the gospel shines, we can be confident that many in heaven belonged to the visible church whose head was the very Antichrist himself. Such is the power of the Holy Spirit working through the gospel!

7. We reject any denial of a bodily resurrection and of the reality and eternity of hell. We reject the teaching that the souls of people who have died return to earth in other bodies (reincarnation) (Hebrews 9:27).

Q: Why do some even within Christianity deny the bodily resurrection of all people?

A: Remember that mere outward membership in the Christian community does not mean that someone is a believer. Much unbelief masquerades under the title "Christianity" this side of heaven. The denial within Christendom of the bodily resurrection is unbelief that springs from the natural skeptical reason of the sinful nature. To our natural human reason, all the truths of the gospel are utterly foolish. "The man without the Spirit does not accept the things that come from the Spirit of God, for they are foolishness to him, and he cannot understand them, because they are spiritually discerned" (1 Corinthians 2:14).

It is significant that Paul wrote those words to the Christians in Corinth. Some in the Corinthian congregation rejected the "foolishness" of the doctrine of the bodily resurrection. Paul wrote about those who rejected the resurrection: "There are some who are ignorant of God" (1 Corinthians 15:34). Unbelief simply cannot fathom that the power of God, which once fashioned humans from the dust, will refashion from the same dust the bodies of those who have died. As Jesus once spoke to those in the church of his day who denied the bodily resurrection, "You are in error because you do not know the Scriptures or the power of God" (Matthew 22:29).

Q: Where does Scripture speak of hell as both real and eternal?

A: One of the clearest passages is Matthew 25:31ff. There Jesus gives us a powerful picture of the great day of judgment as all believers, identified as "the sheep," and all unbelievers, identified as "the goats," are gathered before his throne. As Jesus speaks his words of judgment against the goats, he says, "Depart from me, you who are cursed, into the eternal fire prepared for the devil and his angels" (verse 41). Jesus emphasizes his point at the conclusion of that section: "Then they [the unbelievers] will go away to eternal punishment, but the righteous to eternal life" (verse 46). In this last verse, the reality and eternity of hell is compared to the reality and eternity of heaven.

Q: ∎ **Why do some deny the reality and eternity of hell?**

A: ∎ For many unbelievers, trying to deny the reality and eternity of hell is like whistling in the dark. Their own consciences tell them that they are not right with their Creator. Nevertheless, they desperately try to convince themselves that there is no such thing as a place of eternal judgment for those who reject God. In the words of a popular song from a few decades ago, their motto is: "I swear there ain't no heaven, and I pray there ain't no hell." This denial of hell is just another example of the proud and stubborn sinful human rejection of the Creator's claim on individual life.

Some within the Christian community believe that they must salvage God's reputation by declaring that a loving God could never condemn a person he created to an eternity of suffering apart from his grace and mercy. Ignoring what Scripture clearly says about the reality and eternity of hell, they try to teach only a temporary punishment or an instantaneous annihilation of the unbeliever. Still others suggest the universal salvation of all people. But God has not asked us to apologize for his just judgments. God is both infinite love and infinite justice. Even where his justice may offend our human reason, God remains both perfect love and perfect justice. A God who sent his eternal Son to bleed and die for every last sinner has more than proved his love to the world. His justice also will prove to be perfect when he condemns those who die in unbelief to an eternity in a real hell. No appeals to his judgments and no disagreements will make any sense in the face of his perfect love and justice.

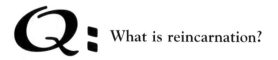

Q: ∎ **What is reincarnation?**

A: Reincarnation—sometimes labeled the "transmigration of souls"—is the belief that our souls live a repeating series of lives on the earth. Each time we die, our souls come back to live in new bodies as other people, or even as animals or other living creatures. The idea that we can develop good karma by leading righteous lives is often connected to the idea of reincarnation. Good karma enables us to come back as higher and higher forms of life. The goal of reincarnation is often expressed as finally breaking the cycle completely. Once that happens, the individual becomes nothing but a pure soul, since material things are evil or nothing but illusion.

Q: **Where does Scripture reject reincarnation?**

A: Reincarnation is a doctrine by which you work your way up the ladder of existence until you leave behind the evil physical body and merge as a pure soul with the impersonal, divine lifeforce. The doctrine makes spiritual completion or acceptance depend on human effort in the various stages or cycles of reincarnation. Such a teaching flies in the face of more doctrines of Scripture than we can list here.

Simply, reincarnation denies the basic biblical teaching that we live once in this life and then face eternity. We learn that from Hebrews 9:27, which says, "Man is destined to die once, and after that to face judgment."

Reincarnation also denies that we rise from the dead on the Last Day. Scripture says that we rise not as someone else but as ourselves, having the same combination of body and soul we had when we lived on earth. Listen to Job's confident confession that he, with his same body, would rise from the dead: "I know that my Redeemer lives, and that in the end he will stand upon the earth. And after my skin has been destroyed, yet in my flesh I will see God; I myself will see him with my own eyes—I, and not another. How my heart yearns within me!" (Job 19:25-27).

Finally and most important, reincarnation denies the entire work of Christ in suffering for our sins. Reincarnation rejects the grace of God in Christ and substitutes human effort in achieving union with divinity.

8. We reject all attempts to interpret the New Testament descriptions of Jesus' second coming, of the end of the world, and of the judgment as mere figures of speech for events that take place not at the end of time but within the ongoing history of the world.

Q: Why would someone teach that Jesus' second coming, the end of the world, and the judgment are mere figures of speech?

A: Perhaps they are trying to "defend" God from the ridicule of scoffers who would say that a delay of two thousand years since Jesus' first coming obviously means that any teachings about a visible return or an end of this present world are just so many empty threats. For believers, God's timing and his plans for the end of the world need no such defense. Remember how long the world waited for his first coming. Just as the first coming of Jesus to save us was real and visible, so his second coming to judge the world will be real and visible as well. All that the world values as more important than Jesus Christ will be gone. The only thing that will matter at that moment will be faith in the Savior's life, death, and resurrection.

Instead of reinterpreting real promises of Scripture as nothing but word pictures, here is the only answer needed: "First of all, you must understand that in the last days scoffers will come, scoffing and following their own evil desires. They will say, 'Where is this "coming" he promised? Ever since our fathers died, everything goes on as it has since the beginning of creation.' But they deliberately forget that long ago by God's word the heavens existed and the earth was formed out of water and by water. By these waters also the world of that time was deluged and destroyed. By the same word the present heavens and earth are reserved for fire, being kept for the day of judgment and destruction of ungodly men. But do not forget this one thing, dear friends: With the Lord a day is like a thousand years, and a thousand years are like a day. The Lord is not slow in keeping his promise, as some understand slowness. He is patient with you, not wanting anyone to perish, but everyone to come to repentance" (2 Peter 3:3-9).

This is what we believe, teach, and confess.

Additional Reading for This Section:

We Believe in Jesus Christ: Essays on Christology edited by Curtis A. Jahn
When Christians Face Death by George R. Brueggemann

Subject Index